WITHDRAWN

Song Dialects and Demes in Sedentary Populations of the White-Crowned Sparrow
(Zonotrichia leucophrys nuttalli)

SONG DIALECTS AND DEMES IN SEDENTARY POPULATIONS OF THE WHITE-CROWNED SPARROW (*ZONOTRICHIA LEUCOPHRYS NUTTALLI*)

BY

LUIS FELIPE BAPTISTA

UNIVERSITY OF CALIFORNIA PRESS
BERKELEY · LOS ANGELES · LONDON

University of California Publications in Zoology

Volume 105
Approved for publication June 14, 1974
Issued November 15, 1975

University of California Press
Berkeley and Los Angeles
California

◆

University of California Press, Ltd.
London, England

591.08
C153u
v.105
1975

ISBN:0−520−09522−7
Library of Congress Catalog Card Number: 74-620115
© 1976 the regents of the university of california
printed in the united states of america

To my father
Cezar Octoviano Baptista,
who introduced me to
the world of birds

CONTENTS

Introduction. 1
Acknowledgments. 2
Methods and Materials 2
    Terminology. 4
    Symbols Used. 5
Some Aspects of White-crown Song 5
    Subsong 5
    Repertoire Size and Matching of Song Themes with Neighbors. 6
    Female Song 9
General Description of the Song of *Nuttalli* 12
    Variation in the Songs of Individual Birds 12
    Variation in Song Length, Frequency and Complexity (Syllable Types)
        Within and Between Populations 14
Morphological Variation in Song 19
    East San Francisco Bay Populations 19
        Distribution of White-crowns in Tilden Park and Berkeley. 19
        Tilden Park populations 20
        The Berkeley populations 21
        Berkeley: subdialects and secondary contact areas. 24
        Brooks Island populations 27
        Richmond secondary contact zone 29
    West San Francisco Bay Populations 30
        City of San Francisco. 30
        Presidio populations 33
        Lake Merced populations 35
        The Treasure Island populations 37
        Fort Baker, Marin County, populations 38
Discussion and Conclusions. 39
    The Evolution of Song Dialects 39
        The role of dispersal 39
        The role of barriers. 40
        The accumulation of cultural micromutations in song 41
        Errors in learning 41
        Improvisation. 42
        The role of inadequate instruction 42
        The role of countersinging 43
    On White-crown Dialects and Panmixia 43
    The Possible Functions of Dialects 45
Summary. 46
Literature Cited 48
Figures 53

SONG DIALECTS AND DEMES IN SEDENTARY POPULATIONS OF THE WHITE-CROWNED SPARROW (*ZONOTRICHIA LEUCOPHRYS NUTTALLI*)

BY

LUIS FELIPE BAPTISTA

(A contribution from the Museum of Vertebrate Zoology of the University of California Berkeley)

Introduction

THE WHITE-CROWNED SPARROW *(Zonotrichia leucophrys)* is the white rat of the ornithological world. A wealth of information has been published concerning various aspects of the biology of this species: systematics, studied by Banks (1964), detailed life history studies by Blanchard (1936, 1941, 1942; see also DeWolfe, 1968), various aspects of physiology by several authors (e.g., Blanchard, 1941; Blanchard and Erickson, 1949; see also review in Mewaldt et al., 1968), Zugunruhe studies have been conducted (see references in Mewaldt et al., 1968) and Marler and Tamura (1962, 1964) have described in some detail several song dialects of the sedentary subspecies *nuttalli* of the White-crowned Sparrow. Although much more experimental work is needed, Marler and his associates (Marler and Tamura, 1964; Marler, 1967a, 1967b, 1970a, 1970b; Marler and Hamilton, 1966; Konishi, 1965) have also studied various aspects of song learning in this species, trying to elucidate the roles of genome and environment in shaping these vocalizations. This impressive body of information, added to the fact that the White-crowned Sparrow can be locally an abundant species, providing large sample sizes for the investigator, makes it an ideal subject for various population studies.

Four, or sometimes five, geographical races of the White-crowned Sparrow are currently recognized (Banks, 1964; Cortopassi and Mewaldt, 1965). The subspecies *nuttalli* breeds in coastal California from about Cape Mendocino to Santa Barbara; banding studies have shown this race to be non-migratory (Blanchard, 1941, 1942). The investigation reported herein is based on populations of the sedentary form *nuttalli* resident in the San Francisco Bay Area of California (see insert in map, fig. 1).

My interest in the White-crown is in the primary song, which I have endeavored to use to study interactions between adjacent populations in the following manner. Marler and Tamura (1962, 1964) have shown that a local population (deme) of White-crowned Sparrows may be recognized by a song pattern characteristic of that area. They have further shown that these song patterns are learned (Marler and Tamura, 1964) and Marler (1970a, 1970b) has found that song learning is restricted to a "critical period" between the age of 10 and 50 days. Blanchard (1941) revealed that the juveniles remain with their parents until approximately day 48. This implies a good correlation between the termination of the critical period of song learning and the time of dispersal so that a dispersed juvenile would bring with it the song or songs it had acquired in its natal area. A detailed study of song variation in local populations should thus enable us to determine:

1. Whether or not gene flow between demes occurs using song as an indicator.

2. What occurs in contact zones between neighboring populations (demes), if and when they do meet. For example, would one find a narrow mixed zone of song themes in such areas, or does one song type drop out in clinal fashion as another comes in?

Author's present address: Moore Laboratory of Zoology, Occidental College, Los Angeles, California 90041.

3. What constitutes "barriers," major and minor, between these populations, if barriers indeed exist. Data may also be gathered on the relative abundance of individuals in relation to ecological features.

4. Where feasible, data may be gathered on the number of birds in a dialect group, or the geographical limits of a dialect in terms of what surface area it may cover.

5. Since during the fall and winter months migrant populations of the races *pugetensis* and *gambelii* mingle with the sedentary *nuttalli,* I wished to know of possible effects of dialects of visiting migrants on the songs of local populations.

Acknowledgments

I thank Dr. Ned K. Johnson, who suggested the problem, for his interest and guidance throughout the course of this study. Drs. Herbert Baker and George Barlow read drafts of the manuscript and offered valuable comments. Dr. Barbara DeWolfe and Michael Faran made their field notes available to me. Dr. Robert Payne permitted me to cite portions of his then unpublished manuscript on song dialects of viduines. Dr. Lewis Petrinovich accompanied me in the field. Fred McCollum also accompanied me in the field and provided fruitful discussion of my material. Dr. William Z. Lidicker provided transportation to Brooks Island. I thank all my friends at the Museum of Vertebrate Zoology for making my stay there such a memorable one. My thanks also to all my friends at the Point Reyes Bird Observatory, especially Dr. Richard Mewaldt, C. John Ralph, John Smail and Robert Stewart for all the courtesies extended me during the course of my studies at that field station. Mrs. Christine Remedios typed the first draft of this manuscript and Mrs. Joanna Rosario prepared the final copy. Field work was made possible by grants from the Chapman Memorial Fund of the American Museum of Natural History, the Chancellor's Patent Fund of the University of California, and travel funds from the Museum of Vertebrate Zoology.

Last but not least my thanks to my wife Joyce for her patience, delightful companionship and assistance in the field, in editing the manuscript, and for providing the computer data analysis without which this study would have been a gargantuan task indeed.

Methods and Materials

Songs were recorded in the field using an Uher 4000 Report-S tape recorder and an Uher microphone mounted on a twenty-four inch parabolic reflector. Tape speed was 7.5 inches per second. Tapes were analyzed in the laboratory using an Ampex tape recorder and a Kay Electric Company Model 6061A Sonograph Machine set at high shape and wide band settings.

The study areas include: (1) the City of Berkeley, Alameda County, California; (2) Tilden Park, Contra Costa County, California; (3) the neighboring cities of Albany, Alameda County, California; (4) El Cerrito, and (5) Richmond, Contra Costa County, California; (6) Brooks Island in the San Francisco Bay a quarter mile off the Richmond shoreline; (7) Treasure Island in the San Francisco Bay; (8) the San Francisco Peninsula, a transect having been made from the Presidio to Lake Merced, San Francisco County, California; (9) Fort Baker at the north end of the Golden Gate Bridge and directly opposite the City of San Francisco; (10) Carmel and Point Lobos, Monterey County, California. Sample sizes for each population in terms of number of birds and number of song spectrograms per population are summarized in table 1. The four individuals from Pt. Reyes referred to in table 1 were outside the study areas. They were however included in this study in that they aided in illustrating the phenomenon of song misimprinting, discussed at length in earlier papers (Baptista, 1973, 1974). The material from Carmel and Point Lobos was also outside the study area. It was included in my treatment of variation in song length. Descriptions of these songs will be included in a paper on geographical variation in song of the migratory subspecies *pugetensis,* with which themes from Carmel and Point Lobos are convergent (Blanchard, 1941).

TABLE 1

Number of Song Spectrograms

	No. of birds	Range	Number of Spectrograms Median	Total
Tilden	58	1-35	8.25	424
Berkeley[a]	115	1-45	5.57	763
Brooks Island	38	1-10	2.94	106
Richmond	3	3-10	5.00	18
Presidio	27	1-21	7.00	193
San Francisco	64	1-26	7.50	448
Lake Merced	61	1-15	3.67	282
Treasure Island	20	1-9	4.25	81
Fort Baker	11	2-12	3.67	59
Point Reyes[b]	4	1-15	1.83	18
Carmel[c]	13	1-10	1.88	28
Total	414	1-45	4.37	2,420

[a]Includes Berkeley, Albany, El Cerrito and Richmond (see map, fig. 1).
[b]Point Reyes Bird Observatory, Marin County, California (see Baptista, 1974).
[c]Includes neighboring Point Lobos, Monterey County.

Whenever possible, a series of at least 10 songs from each bird were spectrographed. In this way something could be said about individual variation in the morphology of components from song to song. Using a table of random numbers, two individuals represented by 10 spectrograms each were selected and the components of each spectrogram analyzed and compared in order to have some idea of variation in some of the temporal and frequency parameters of the song. Otherwise the longest and clearest spectrogram from each bird's recorded repertoire was selected for analysis of these characters. With all these data taken together, I hoped to have some idea of individual variation, intra-population or intra-dialect variation, and variation between dialects. Hopefully, this would permit discussion of species specific parameters governing White-crown song. Although this report concerns mostly the songs and behavior of populations of the race *nuttalli* of the White-crowned Sparrow permanently resident in the San Francisco Bay Area, wherever I deem pertinent, reference will be made also to songs and behavior of other populations of *nuttalli* as well as to representatives of the race *pugetensis* which I have studied (Baptista, 1974, and in preparation).

A pilot study was begun in April 1968 when songs were recorded in a transect from the campus of the University of California, Berkeley, through Strawberry Canyon to the crest of the Berkeley Hills and the entrance to Tilden Park. When I found that the Inspiration Point and Berkeley Dialects of Marler and Tamura (1962) existed sympatrically in the Canyon (fig. 1), the project was expanded the following year to include all the study areas mentioned earlier. Data from 1968, 1969, 1970 and 1971 were pooled, but care was taken not to include duplicated material when studying intra-population variation. White-crowns of the subspecies *nuttalli* remain in their established territories even through the winter months (Blanchard, 1936, 1941). Thus, presumably there would be few individuals drifting from one locality to another. In pooling data, only material from different localities in any one study area or new motifs appearing in localities sampled previously were considered. In a few cases the same localities were sampled two to four years in a row to ascertain if any changes occurred in that short span of time. These cases will be discussed in greater detail in later sections.

TERMINOLOGY

Terminology used to describe the components of songs as observed on sound spectrograms follows Marler and Tamura (1962), Marler and Isaac (1961), Mulligan (1966) and Heckenlively (1970).

1. NOTE — any continuous trace on the sound spectrograph.

2. SYLLABLE — the unit of repetition in a trill, consisting of a note or group of notes forming "a more or less coherent unit" (Marler and Isaac, 1961).

3. COMPLEX SYLLABLE — in some dialects (see, e.g., fig. 1, A of Marler and Tamura, 1962) syllables seem to appear in pairs forming a more or less continuous audible unit. In computing the duration of components in songs, I will treat these as single entities. In songs of *pugetensis* (Baptista, 1974) these can be elaborate, each complex syllable made up of more than four notes. Thompson (1968) has described complex elements for various species of *Passerina*.

4. TRILL — syllables repeated one or more times following the whistle or introductory portion of a White-crown song. The pulses of sound emitted may be at a rate of up to 30 per second following the criterion of Borror (1960; *in* Heckenlively, 1970).

5. WHISTLE — a continuous trace on the sound spectrogram generally exceeding 0.2 seconds in duration. They make up the first element of each White-crown song in all spectrograms examined so far. The whistle may be a straight, almost horizontal line on the sound spectrogram, or if frequency modulated may be a wavy line sloping in varying degrees.

6. BUZZ — or VIBRATO of Marler and Tamura (1962). A whistle modulated very rapidly in frequency, e.g., Phrase B of Marler and Tamura's (1962) Inspiration Point (Tilden Park) dialect. Borror (1960) distinguishes a buzz from a trill in that the buzz would contain more than 30 sound pulses per second whereas the trill would not.

7. WHISTLE-BUZZ or BUZZ-WHISTLE — as their names imply consist of these two types of elements attached to each other. Similar elements have been found in songs of Mexican Juncos *(Junco phaeonotus)* by Marler and Isaac (1961).

8. STACCATO PHRASE — replaces in some songs, the whistle or buzz generally constituting the second phrase. A very rapid trill; it is generally of very narrow frequency span, and of the same duration as whistle or buzz phrases. I am therefore treating these

as phrases which I have called staccato phrases (see second phrases in fig. 22, B2 to G).

9. PHRASE — Staccato notes (see 8, above), a Whistle, Buzz or the combination of the two. This term does not include syllables.

10. SONG TYPE — the above listed elements delivered in various permutations and combinations forming coherent units of sound. The terms THEME and MOTIF will be used interchangeably with SONG TYPE to avoid the monotonous repetition of terms.

11. CULTURAL HYBRID SONG — a song containing syllables and/or phrases taken from two distinct themes but combined to make a new theme (see, e.g., fig. 13, C.).

Only four new terms have been introduced in this study; namely, the Complex Syllable, the Staccato Phrase, the Whistle-Buzz and Buzz-Whistle. The last three have not been reported hitherto for White-crowns.

SYMBOLS USED

I have found it useful, especially in comparing dialects or different themes within dialects, to use the following symbols to signify the above elements in describing song. The symbols used are merely the first letter of each term. Thus:

WHISTLE	W	SYLLABLE	S
BUZZ	B	COMPLEX SYLLABLE	CS
WHISTLE-BUZZ	WB	TRILL made up of simple syllables	SS
BUZZ-WHISTLE	BW	Major units of silence	dashes
STACCATO-PHRASE	St		

The use of this system has been demonstrated in a previous paper (Baptista, 1974).

Some Aspects of White-crown Sparrow Song
SUBSONG

In the laboratory, Marler (1970a) found that hand-raised White-crowns kept in individual isolation did not come into song until about 8 months of age. Song was not crystallized until about 12 months of age. Hand-raised birds in group isolation came into song at 2 to 3 months of age and song was reported to crystallize more rapidly. Marler (1970a) has suggested that "lack of general social stimulation" as a result of the first group being individually isolated may account for the slower timing of events. Rice and Thompson (1968) found that hand-raised Indigo Buntings *(Passerina cyanea)* isolated individually "sang very little and very irregularly." Sounds from a radio piped into the cage "increased the frequency of singing somewhat." One individual never sang during its 16 months confinement in a sound-proof cage and began to do so only when placed in a room with ordinary household noises. With those buntings, birds commenced singing from 15 to 60 days of age.

In the field, Blanchard (1941) found in the subspecies *nuttalli* of the White-crowned Sparrow that: "The young birds begin to sing, though rarely, in mid-July, while still in Juvenile plumage." On July 27, 1969, I observed a flock of about 10 *nuttalli* in juvenile plumage foraging in a grassy area north of the Palace of the Legion of Honor, San Francisco, California. One of these was observed to sing a few notes of subsong. On August 16, 1969, I was studying White-crowns at the Point Reyes Bird Observatory, about four miles north of Bolinas, California. At this late date there were few adults singing. I tried to stimulate song by playing some tapes of White-crown themes and elicited a bout of what was apparently very plastic subsong from a juvenile. On August 25, in the backyard of my home in San Francisco, I witnessed a bout of approximately fifteen minutes of countersinging between an adult and a juvenile in very plastic subsong. The songs of the adult were stereotyped, though they often lacked some of the terminal syllables in the trill. Songs of the juvenile sometimes consisted of an introductory whistle followed by a buzz, and then a trill as in the White-crown songs of this neighborhood. Sometimes the buzz in the middle was lacking. At other times the trill was followed by a series of amorphous whistles, which did not sound like any elements sung by the local White-crowns. Nonetheless, the division of each of its songs into a whistle and a trill portion suggested that this individual's songs were on the way to crystallization. Blanchard (1941: 17-18) described similar features of subsong in this species and reported hearing juveniles singing like adults as early as November. Others were heard in subsong as late in winter as January 9. She (page 14) also observed a bout of countersinging similar to the one described above between an adult and an immature on August 30, 1936.

On May 14, 1969, on the corner of Cragmont and Spruce Avenues, Berkeley, I recorded a White-crown singing a bout of very plastic song in the shadow of an ornamental *Cedrus deodora.* Its plumage was that of an adult, including a black and white crown. I recorded and spectrographed a series of thirteen songs, three of which are illustrated in Baptista (1972c) along with a normal *nuttalli* song for comparison. The morphology and frequency ranges of the elements as illustrated are variable. Moreover the songs were sung softly and were never complete. These motifs bear almost all the features Thorpe and Pilcher (1958) outlined as characterizing subsong. Subsong at such a late date is certainly extraordinary and merits explanation.

The physiological effect of testosterone in controlling the onset of song in fringillids has been demonstrated for the White-crown by Konishi (1965) and by Nottebohm (1969a) for the Chaffinch *(Fringilla coelebs).* Nottebohm (1969a) castrated a young male Chaffinch in January and found that it never produced subsong or song even when given a regime of 16 hours daylight. When this individual was implanted the following spring with a 10 mg. pellet of testosterone proprionate, it eventually came into subsong. Konishi (1965) has further shown that a young male White-crown implanted with a testosterone pellet in its first fall, before the onset of subsong, came into full song. The abnormal songs of the White-crown discussed above could be explained as possibly the result of hormonal malfunctioning in the late winter or early spring when most yearlings first come into song. It is possible that at the time I recorded its songs its male hormones were beginning to flow normally, inducing late onset of song in this individual. A second possible explanation for this individual's rather abnormal songs is that they were sung by a female. These songs certainly bear some of the features Blanchard (1941; see also the section below on female song) outlined for songs of female White-crowns and Falls (1969) for songs of female White-throated Sparrows (*Zonotrichia albicollis*).

REPERTOIRE SIZE AND MATCHING OF SONG THEMES WITH NEIGHBORS

Some investigators have reported that White-crowns are predisposed to sing one theme (Marler, 1970a). Most of the White-crowns sampled in the San Francisco Bay Area sang one theme each. However, 17 individuals, or 4.2%, of the Bay Area sample sang more than one song type (table 2).

TABLE 2
Repertoire Sizes of nuttalli Sampled

	No. of birds	1	2	3	4
Tilden	58	57	—	1[c]	—
Berkeley	115	108	5	1	1[c]
Brooks Island	39	38	1[b]	—	—
Richmond	3	3	—	—	—
Presidio	27	25	2	—	—
San Francisco	64	63	1	—	—
Lake Merced	61	56	5	—	—
Treasure Island	20	20	—	—	—
Fort Baker	11	11	—	—	—
Point Reyes	4[a]	3	—	1[c]	—
Total	402	384	14	3	1

(Number of themes sung: columns 1–4)

[a] Point Reyes Bird Observatory, Marin County, California.
[b] Data from McCollum (personal communication).
[c] Data from Baptista (1974).

Earlier (Baptista, 1974) I reported on six individuals belonging to the subspecies *nuttalli* that sang from one to three *pugetensis* themes. A seventh bird sang two *nuttalli* themes, a *pugetensis* song, and a fourth theme combining syllables from both *pugetensis* and *nuttalli* songs. Several factors were suggested that might control repertoire size in the individual White-crown. Herein are presented data on multi-themed birds that sang only *nuttalli* themes. The singing behavior of these individuals are described and evidence presented for the phenomenon of countersinging which probably influences the sample sizes of multi-themed individuals encountered by the investigator in the field.

I have one record of a bird in El Cerrito, California, singing three motifs (fig. 6) each of these being sung by several other individuals within earshot (fig. 5). Thirteen individuals belonging to the subspecies *nuttalli* recorded within the study areas reported here sang two motifs each. McCollum (personal communication) heard a White-crown singing two distinct themes on Brooks Island in the San Francisco Bay.

Outside of the San Francisco Bay Area, I have records of four other birds singing two song patterns in the vicinity of the Point Reyes Bird Observatory, 3 miles north of Bolinas, California. One bird sang three themes (Baptista, 1974). I heard but did not record a bird singing two motifs at the western end of the Bear Valley Trail, Point Reyes, Marin County, California. A bird recorded at Point Lobos, Monterey County, California, sang two themes (Baptista, 1972c).

In a survey of geographical variation in song in the migratory White-crowned Sparrow *Zonotrichia leucophrys pugetensis* (Baptista, 1974, and in preparation) I found that most individuals sang one theme each, but a few sang two. Banks (1964: 18) reported on one bird that sang three themes. DeWolfe et al. (1974) reported on a few members of the subspecies *gambelii* that sang two themes.

There appears to be species specific differences in the way birds order song themes in a singing bout. I found that a White-crown singing more than one motif would usually alternate a bout of one with a bout of the other, then a bout of the first, and so on. This is the more common method of song delivery, and has been reported for Chaffinches *(Fringilla coelebs)* by Hinde (1958), Thorpe (1958) and Marler (1956), for the Oregon Junco *(Junco oreganus)* by Konishi (1964), for various members of the genus *Passerina* by Thompson (1968), for Cardinals *(Richmondena cardinalis)* by Lemon (1967), to name a few species. I have never found any individual alternating two song types in perfect sequence as Davis (1958: 315) reported for some Rufous-sided Towhees *(Pipilo erythrophthalmus)*, Heckenlively (1970) for Black-throated Sparrows *(Amphispiza bilineata)*, or Yellowhammers *(Emberiza citrinella)* and Cuban Melodious Grassquits *(Tiaris canora)* (Baptista, personal observation).

In the individual repertoire, the proportions of each song type in a bout of song may vary considerably from day to day and even for different parts of the day (see also the history of bird P4, Baptista, 1974). For example, on April 14, 1969, I recorded 23 songs from a bird at Kenyon and Lake Drive, Berkeley. Twenty-two of these songs had whistles making up the second phrase (see fig. 6, E) and only the fourteenth song in the recorded series had a buzz in place of the whistle (fig. 6, E1). Thereafter I heard many songs from this individual but did not hear it sing any more buzz songs. On April 18 I returned to this spot and this time a bird (probably the same one) was alternating short bouts of each song type. I tried to get it to match each of my tape recorded song themes, but was unsuccessful. On March 3 and 4 I heard a bird in the courtyard of the Boalt Law School, University of California, Berkeley, singing a long bout of predominantly buzz songs of the type described above, with only occasional whistle songs. On March 21 a bird here (probably the same one) sang a long series of whistle songs. Only one buzz song was heard on this day. On March 24 this individual was singing a bout of predominantly whistle songs when I arrived at 6:50 a.m. I played a buzz song and it immediately changed from a series of whistle songs, replying to my taped song with a bout of buzz songs, followed by alternating bouts of each song theme. I was able to make it match my tape recorded buzz songs with bouts of buzz songs in five other such trials. On March 24 I repeated this experiment and in six out of seven trials it matched my taped buzz song with a series of like songs. Although on the seventh trial the immediate reply was a whistle song, this was followed by a series of nine buzz songs, in contrast to a bout of seventeen whistle songs which preceded the buzz song played to it. This bird was not seen again on March 26 or thereafter, thus terminating the possibility of further experiments with it.

On April 8, 1970, I discovered yet another bird singing both a whistle and a vibrato song in El Cerrito, California. I watched it match a neighbor with a buzz song and still another with a whistle song. In four trials it matched my tape recorded buzz songs and in two others my whistle songs. Two more birds with bivalent repertoires, one recorded on April 10, 1970, and the other on April 28 on the east shore of Lake Merced, San Francisco, were heard matching their two song types with neighbors as well as with songs from my tape recorder. A bird recorded at Crescent City, Del Norte County, California, on June 6, 1970, and therefore belonging to the race *pugetensis* (by geographic locality) sang two different themes. It was also induced to match each of its tape-recorded song types played back to it.

Four other birds I experimented with could not be persuaded to match my tape-recorded song themes. It is possible that these individuals were perturbed by background noises in the tape, by poor recordings, and in at least one case by a heavy flow of auto traffic in the neighborhood. They were possibly thus in conflict between replying to playback or avoiding the "strange sounds and sights."

I have found a vast amount of individual variation in responses of White-crowns with song repertoires of normal size (namely one) to tape-recorded songs. Some would fly away whereas others were so aggressive as to actually approach and perch on the tape recorder, sometimes pecking at it when it heard a song, as Verner and Milligan (1971) also observed. It should not be too surprising then that only some White-crowns could be persuaded to match tape-recorded songs. Although more experiments are in order, the data above, including three field observations of "undisturbed" birds in nature, suggest that White-crowns with several themes in their repertoires often tend to match these in bouts of counter-singing. The Rufous-sided Towhee *(Pipilo erythrophthalmus)* which was studied by Davis (1958) in California, often had more than one theme in each bird's repertoire, but song matching was not observed. However, the population studied by Kroodsma (1971) in Oregon tended to match song types in bouts of counter-singing. Roberts (1969; cited in Kroodsma, 1971) was able to induce this behavior in playback experiments. Song matching in the field has been reported for a number of other species such as the Bewick's Wren *(Thryomanes bewicki)* by Kroodsma (1971), the Black-crested Titmouse *(Parus atricristatus)* by Lemon (1968), the Plain Titmouse *(Parus inornatus)* by Dixon (1969), the Cardinal *(Richmondena cardinalis)* by Lemon (1967) and the Chaffinch *(Fringilla coelebs)* by Marler (1956). Hinde (1958) studied the Chaffinch in the laboratory; although in his experiments actual song matching was not achieved, he showed that, "When the singing is in some measure a response to a stimulus song type from the bird's own repertoire, the proportion of that song type tends to increase." Marler (1960) has suggested that counter-singing of this type may serve to preserve certain themes in any one area. Themes less often used are forgotten, as it were, and thus lost.

Repertoire size seems to be similar in two of the White-crown's congeners, namely the White-throated Sparrow *(Zonotrichia albicollis)* and the Rufous-collared Sparrow *(Zonotrichia capensis).* Falls (1969) found that although each male White-throated Sparrow "typically sings a single stereotyped pattern," a few birds were found to have a second motif of a different pattern which was less often used. Borror and Gunn (1965) sampled the songs of 711 White-throats and found only 15 individuals singing two patterns. Miller and Miller (1968) studied the Rufous-collared Sparrow in Columbia and found that: "One individual may have two to four slightly different patterns but this is not usual, nor does one hear a male with alternate patterns shift frequently from one to another." Nottebohm (1969b) reported on the songs of 523 individuals; 17 of these individuals sang two themes each and 2 had repertoires of three themes each.

FEMALE SONG

Blanchard (1941: 14), studying color banded individuals, described the song of the female White-crown as, "identical in pattern with that of the male but is usually fainter, more rapidly uttered, and often incomplete." She added (page 20) that "her weak song, which continues until nesting time, is not used for advertisement or warning, as is the loud song of her mate." Blanchard (1941: 14) described one exception however. This was a female that was observed on September 17, 1935, to engage a neighboring male in a four or five minute bout of countersinging as the result of a dispute over some berries. She was "singing as forcefully as any male in breeding time." Elsewhere (Blanchard, 1936, 1941:20;

see also De Wolfe, 1968 and Nice, 1941) she described a case of polygyny in which a male was mated to two females, so that with the approach of reproduction, "each female created for herself a subdivision of the main territory which she defended against the other female by loud singing and fighting, and in which she finally chose her nest site." Skirmishes at territorial boundaries and song duels between the two females were observed on later occasions as well. She also stated (Blanchard, 1936: 149) that "had they not been banded, I should have thought I was watching a boundary dispute between two males."

To Blanchard's field data I may add a record of what I believe to be both members of a mated pair replying to playback with song. On the evening of March 23, 1969, I was attracted to a White-crown on Seventeenth Avenue and Clement Street, San Francisco, California, singing a song which was rather unusual for this area in that it lacked the buzz (Phrase B of Marler and Tamura, 1962) which is characteristic of most of the birds in this part of San Francisco. I returned the next morning and with playback attracted two birds, both singing songs with only one whistle in the introduction (W-SS) (spectrogram in Baptista, 1972c). They kept changing their singing posts, both singing at me from the roof tops, telephone poles and a tall palm tree in the neighborhood. I recorded a series of songs from one of the birds (the male?). Soon the two birds began to forage a few feet apart on one of the front yards, and I was able to record three incomplete songs from the second individual (the female?) which sang between bouts of foraging. They seemed to be the only two White-crowns on this block. I came again to this area on March 24th and got more recordings from what was probably the first bird; at least the spectrograms were identical to those recorded on the first occasion. Another bird was with it trilling sporadically, but no more song was heard from it.

The spectrograms for the two birds showed some distinct differences. Firstly, the structure of the initial two syllables in each of their trills differed morphologically. Secondly, the whistles introducing the male's songs were stereotyped, and were somewhat straighter than the wavy whistles of the female.

Singing behavior in the female White-crown seems to be similar in many respects to that of the White-throated Sparrow *(Zonotrichia albicollis)* studied by Falls (1969) and his colleagues. Females of the latter species "sometimes sing spontaneously early in the breeding season and often give a few songs in response to playback" (Falls, 1969:210). Sound spectrograms revealed differences between male and female song in that female songs are often "short, quavering and variable in speed. . . [and] lack the precise control of pitch and timing characteristic of males." He suggested also that these qualities in female song may be a function of hormone level, because birds treated in the laboratory with testosterone sang songs like those of territorial males. Female songs used in playback experiments, elicited weaker responses from males (Falls, 1969).

Song from female White-crowns, has been induced in the laboratory with testosterone injections (Konishi, 1965; Kern and King, 1972; Baptista, 1974). There appears to be some differences between the females' songs and similar themes sung by territorial males in all these cases. On the other hand, Konishi (1965) treated a young male with testosterone and found that it "developed a good copy of the dialect of the area from which it came." It is still not known whether or not females, given longer periods of hormone treatment, and therefore longer "practice" sessions, could improve their singing capabilities to match those of territorial males. The softer, often incomplete themes sung by female *nuttalli* in the field (Blanchard, 1941; this study) are probably due to lower (more normal) hormone levels than those to which birds were subjected in the laboratory.

Female song in White-crowned Sparrows and White-throated Sparrows seems to be confined, under normal conditions, to the early part of the breeding season (Blanchard, 1941; Kern and King, 1972; personal observation). Kern and King (1972:207) have suggested a number of possible functions for song in female *Zonotrichia,* including solidifying the pair-bond, stimulating the breeding activities of the male, and possibly ensuring "reproductive isolation between regional populations if the female recognizes the males of her own group by their song pattern (Nottebohm, 1970), and vice versa." Some differences between male and female song in the field would also be desirable, in that these may serve to identify sex.

Kern and King (1972: 207-208) pointed out that androgens have been identified in the avian ovary and in avian blood, and that these hormones normally participate in the development of the avian oviduct. They also stated that ovarian estrogens are synthesized from androgens, and that perhaps (page 208) "androgenic effects may be externalized as song."

Because tape-recorded song evokes aggressive behavior from territory holding males, it is probably of adaptive significance that spontaneous, female song is confined to the early part of the breeding season. At this time males are less aggressive and respond weakly if at all to playback of recorded song. This is probably due to low androgen levels. A female singing as loudly as her mate through the breeding season is likely to be taken for an encroaching male as illustrated by the following incident: At 8:30 p.m. on May 28, 1969, I observed a White-crown feeding on a lawn on the University of California, Berkeley campus. A second individual was singing from a tree directly overhead. I played a loud White-crown song and the feeding bird trilled in response. The singing individual however immediately swooped down on the first, seized it by the rectrices, while it struggled to get away. The second bird then let go of its hold. They stood looking at each other a few seconds, and then foraged side by side on the grass. This was apparently a mated pair.

Miller and Miller (1968) studied the biology of a congener, the Rufous-collared or Andean Sparrow *(Zonotrichia capensis)* in Colombia. Females of that species were not observed to sing in the field. However, a captive female sang a song "somewhat subdued and rapid compared with that of males." Nottebohm (1972) studying the same species in Argentina reported that, "Female chingolos also sing, but as pairs form and occupy territories, female singing is probably suppressed." Nice (1943) studied singing behavior in the related Song Sparrow *(Melospiza melodia).* In that species female song was rare and was "confined to that period in early spring before nest building" began. This behavior is reminiscent of females of the three species of *Zonotrichia* discussed earlier.

Female song was reported for the Orange-billed Sparrow *(Arremon aurantiirostris)* by Skutch (1954; see also Thorpe, 1964). There appears to be differences in male and female songs in this species also. In contrast to all the species discussed earlier, however, female song is not restricted to the period before breeding; females even sing while incubating eggs (Skutch, 1954). Roberts (1969) studied vocalizations of the Rufous-sided Towhee *(Pipilo erythrophthalmus).* In that species birds (sexes unknown) studied in the field sang both loud and whisper songs. A captive male sang both song types. A captive female sang only quiet songs, and in contrast to the male's songs, hers were always "amorphous, complex, and never followed any consistent pattern." Once again there appears to be differences between male and female song which may function in sexual recognition.

General Description of the Song of Nuttalli

A song of the sedentary White-crown is about 2 seconds long, and may be divided into an introductory portion (consisting of one, two, or three phrases) followed by a trill portion made up of syllables repeated in a series (Marler and Tamura 1962, 1964; this study). In some populations, notably in parts of Marin County (Marler and Tamura, 1964), in Lake Merced, San Francisco (figs. 21 and 22) and in Carmel, Monterey County, California (Blanchard, 1941; Peterson, 1941; Baptista, 1972c), songs have an additional terminal buzz or staccato phrase.

Songs of the migratory subspecies *pugetensis* may likewise be divided into an introductory and a trill portion (Baptista 1974, and in preparation). However, songs of the migratory form *gambelii* (Blanchard and Erickson, 1949; Peyton and DeWolfe, 1968; DeWolfe et al., 1974) and the eastern subspecies *leucophrys* (Borror, 1961) do not appear to have the long trills of the two Pacific Coast subspecies. The spectrograms illustrated in Borror (1961:165) for *leucophrys* and that for *gambelii* by DeWolfe et al. (1974:230) are remarkably similar. Both songs begin with a whistle, followed by a short warbled section, then two buzzes and finally a short trill.

Based on external morphology, taxonomists recognize two racial complexes for the White-crowned Sparrow (Banks, 1964; Cortopassi and Mewaldt, 1965). Birds belonging to the *nuttalli-pugetensis* group of the Pacific Coast are darker than the *gambelii-leucophrys-oriantha* complex. The published spectrograms suggest that *gambelii* song is quite similar to *leucophrys,* but both are easily differentiated from songs of *nuttalli-pugetensis.* Song may prove a good taxonomic character separating the two racial complexes.

DeWolfe et al. (1974) found no evidence of song dialects in *gambelii* as has been described for *nuttalli* (Marler and Tamura, 1962, 1964; this study) and *pugetensis* (Baptista, 1974).

VARIATION IN THE SONGS OF INDIVIDUAL BIRDS

Using a table of random numbers, 2 birds singing Berkeley themes (Berkeley birds were the best represented) were selected for analysis of individual variation within song themes. Visual inspection of sound spectrograms of the songs of over 400 White-crowns revealed an impressive uniformity with regard to morphology, and to permutations and combinations of syllables and phrases within a series of songs, from any song bout. Marler and Tamura (1962) and DeWolfe et al. (1974) made similar observations for the songs of *nuttalli* and *gambelii* respectively. Thus the first ten cleanest song spectrograms from a singing bout of each of the two randomly selected individuals were used to analyze variation in the following song characteristics:

1. Number of syllables, as counted on the spectrogram.
2. Number of elements (number of syllables plus number of phrases).
3. Number of kinds of elements, i.e, kinds of syllables plus kinds of phrases, based on morphology.
4. Repetition index, i.e., 2 above divided by 3.
5. Total length of the song measured to the nearest centisecond.
6. Trill length, i.e., the length of the portion of song immediately following the introduction, measured to the nearest centisecond.
7. Highest frequency of all syllables, i.e, one of each syllable type was selected randomly and pooled. These were measured to the nearest 0.25 KHz.

8. Lowest frequency of all syllables. Syllables were selected as in 7, above, and pooled.

The measurements were of course subject to all the sources of error discussed by Marler and Isaac (1960) in their analysis of songs of the Chipping Sparrow *(Spizella passerina)*.

Data are summarized in table 3. The small standard deviations attest to the stereotypy of the characteristics analyzed.

TABLE 3

Bird No. 315, from El Cerrito, California, Spectrogram in Fig. 6, A1

	N	Range	Mean	SD
Syllables	10	10-12	10.60	±0.70
Elements	10	12-14	12.60	±0.70
Kinds of elements	10	5-5	5	±0
Repetition index	10	2.40-2.80	2.52	±0.14
Trill length	10	0.97-1.15	1.03	±0.059
Song length	10	1.87-2.07	1.94	±0.065
Highest frequency (kHz)	10	6.75-7.50	6.95	±0.23
Lowest frequency (kHz)	10	2.00-2.50	2.22	±0.14

Bird No. 299, from Albany, California, Spectrograms in Fig. 4, H and H1

	N	Range	Mean	SD
Syllables	10	12-13	12.30	±0.48
Elements	10	13-14	13.30	±0.48
Kinds of elements	10	5-5	5	±0
Repetition index	10	2.60-2.80	2.66	±0.097
Trill length	10	1.12-1.20	1.15	±0.033
Song length	10	1.67-1.80	1.73	±0.045
Highest frequency (kHz)	10	6.50-7.00	6.72	±0.14
Lowest frequency (kHz)	10	2.00-2.25	2.10	±0.13

Two spectrograms selected from the repertoire of Bird 299 are illustrated in figure 4, H and H1. In song H, there are two terminal flourishes ending at a lower frequency than the other syllables in the trill. In song H1, the penultimate syllable is slurred up, joining the upper portion of the terminal flourish. I do not consider these two terminal portions (as seen in H and H1) within the normal range of variation for this individual. They were never repeated in its song bout, the rest of its song ending with terminal syllables as seen in songs E to G, figure 4. Other than this, morphological variation in the songs of birds 315 and 299 (table 3) was of the type described by Marler and Tamura (1962), namely in varying the introduction length or the number of syllables in the trill.

A bird singing four themes (see spectrograms of bird P4 in Baptista, 1974: 157-158) was captured and given the freedom of my home. Song spectrograms of themes recorded in the field on April 27, 1971, were compared with themes recorded in my home on March 9 and 10, 1972. No changes in advertising songs were detected. A bird studied in the field (P3 in Baptista, 1974) sang the same theme over three years. These data support the conclusion of Marler and Tamura (1962:370) based on studies of captives, that Whitecrown song and repertoire size are stable once song is crystallized.

VARIATIONS IN SONG LENGTH, FREQUENCY AND COMPLEXITY (SYLLABLE TYPES) WITHIN AND BETWEEN POPULATIONS

Nottebohm (1969b) has suggested that one possible function of song dialects is that it promotes inbreeding in local populations, thus fixing adaptive traits within demes. This would necessitate recognition of home dialects by both sexes, as was indeed demonstrated by Milligan and Verner (1971) for White-crowns. Song dialects of White-crowns are easily distinguishable on the basis of syllable morphology (Marler and Tamura, 1962, 1964; this study). Univariate tests were thus conducted between neighboring dialects that were partially sympatric (e.g., Berkeley and Tilden Park) or potentially so (e.g., Presidio and Fort Baker), to see if differences could be found for each of the characteristics measured. Multivariate tests were decided against since the importance of any one characteristic would be submerged in the vector of variables.

Descriptive statistics for eight characteristics were computed for the nine populations. When the distributions appeared approximately normal, t-tests were conducted for each pair of populations. When the distributions were bimodal, skewed or otherwise non-normal, χ^2 tests were calculated. The numbers of birds used in measuring the characters summarized in tables 4 to 11 differ in each table because song spectrograms were omitted due to lack of clarity in portions of songs as a result of recording artifacts. For example, a spectrogram with the introductory whistle cut off may not be used to measure song length, but may be used to measure trill length, etc. Data for each population are summarized in tables 4 to 11, and tests on each population pair in table 12.

Table 12 shows that neighboring populations may be distinguished by from two to eight variables, which could conceivably be used by birds in dialect recognition. This is in contrast to song dialects of Viduine Finches (*Vidua* spp.) that were readily distinguishable by morphology, but were similar with regard to "song duration, frequency range and song complexity" (Payne, 1973: 138-139).

Mulligan (1963) has called attention to the great significance that temporal patterns may have in behavior. Konishi (1969) subjected auditory neurons of White-crowns to experimentally applied clicks, and found "100 per cent time-locking" when inter-click intervals were only 1.6 milliseconds. It is noteworthy therefore that significant differences in song length were found between three of the population pairs tested (tables 8 and 12), namely Berkeley versus Tilden ($P < .05$), Berkeley versus Brooks ($P < .05$), and San Francisco versus Lake Merced ($P < .005$).

871 Song Sparrow *(Melospiza melodia)* songs measured by Mulligan (1963) ranged from 1.2 to 5.2 seconds, with a mean of slightly over 2.6 seconds. The distribution was approximately normal when plotted on normal probability paper. Song length of 375 White-crowns in this study ranged from 1.50 to 2.81 seconds, with a mean of 2.13 seconds and a standard deviation of 0.22. The distribution of songs in this study was also approximately normal (fig. 25).

Mulligan (1966:55) discussed variation in song length of four North American emberizines. Of the species treated, he found that White-crowns were the least variable in this regard, with a coefficient of variation of 10 versus 18 or 20 for the other forms. Coefficient of variation for the songs of 375 birds in this study was 10.48, comparing favorably with Mulligan's (1966) data.

TABLE 4
Number of Syllables

	N	Range	Mean	SD
Tilden	53	7-15	9.43	1.55
Berkeley	108	8-21	11.82	2.24
Brooks Island	38	4-11	6.84	1.76
Richmond	3	8-11	9.33	1.53
Presidio	28	4-11	7.18	2.02
San Francisco	51	5-13	7.65	1.96
Lake Merced	59	2-7	3.34	0.82
Treasure Island	19	6-15	8.95	2.07
Fort Baker	11	5-12	8.18	1.83

TABLE 5
Number of Elements

	N	Range	Mean	SD
Tilden	53	9-17	11.43	1.55
Berkeley	108	10-22	13.63	2.21
Brooks Island	38	5-12	8.34	1.53
Richmond	3	9-12	10.33	1.53
Presidio	28	6-13	9.21	2.01
San Francisco	51	7-15	9.59	1.89
Lake Merced	59	5-10	6.32	0.84
Treasure Island	19	8-16	10.89	1.91
Fort Baker	11	7-14	10.18	1.83

TABLE 6
Number of Kinds of Elements

	3	4	5	6	7	Total	Mean	SD
Tilden			31	22		53	5.42	0.50
Berkeley		4	49	54		107	5.47	0.57
Brooks Island	5	31	2			38	3.92	0.43
Richmond	3					3	3.00	0
Presidio		25	3			28	4.11	0.31
San Francisco		7	44			51	4.86	0.35
Lake Merced			49	9	1	59	5.19	0.43
Treasure Island		1	16	2		19	5.05	0.40
Fort Baker		4	7			11	4.64	0.50

TABLE 7
Repetition Index

	N	Range	Mean	SD
Tilden	54	1.67-2.80	2.12	0.34
Berkeley	107	1.83-5.50	2.52	0.50
Brooks Island	38	1.67-3.33	2.14	0.40
Richmond	3	3.00-4.00	3.44	0.51
Presidio	28	1.50-3.25	2.25	0.49
San Francisco	51	1.40-3.25	2.00	0.51
Lake Merced	59	1.00-2.00	1.23	0.17
Treasure Island	19	1.60-4.00	2.17	0.49
Fort Baker	11	1.75-2.80	2.20	0.34

TABLE 8
Total Length of the Songs (in seconds)

	N	Range	Mean	SD
Tilden	53	1.83-2.70	2.12	0.18
Berkeley	108	1.50-2.81	2.05	0.26
Brooks Island	38	1.83-2.75	2.17	0.22
Richmond	3	1.99-2.57	2.21	0.31
Presidio	24	1.82-2.61	2.20	0.20
San Francisco	51	1.70-2.81	2.23	0.21
Lake Merced	55	1.76-2.47	2.07	0.16
Treasure Island	19	1.93-2.65	2.30	0.19
Fort Baker	11	1.87-2.40	2.11	0.15

TABLE 9
Trill Length (in seconds)

	N	Range	Mean	SD
Tilden	53	0.78-1.45	0.97	0.14
Berkeley	109	0.75-1.85	1.09	0.20
Brooks Island	38	0.86-1.91	1.23	0.25
Richmond	3	1.30-1.87	1.56	0.29
Presidio	25	0.74-1.54	1.13	0.21
San Francisco	51	0.84-1.84	1.20	0.21
Lake Merced	55	0.78-1.53	1.06	0.14
Treasure Island	19	0.96-1.90	1.30	0.25
Fort Baker	11	0.85-1.30	1.04	0.14

TABLE 10
Highest Frequency of All Syllable Types
(in kHz)

	3.50-	4.00-	4.50-	5.00-	5.50-	6.00-	6.50-	7.00-	7.50-	8.00-	8.50-	Total	Mean	SD
Tilden				13	31	38	37	16	5			140	6.18	0.63
Berkeley		1	8	27	65	43	73	41	8			266	6.16	0.72
Brooks Island		1	9	20	6		16	31	2			85	6.12	0.97
Richmond	1		2					2	1			6	5.79	1.64
Presidio				1	3	6	14	8		1		33	6.52	0.56
San Francisco			3	5	17	28	29	27	12	3	1	125	6.49	0.78
Lake Merced						13	40	43	17	7		120	6.99	0.47
Treasure Island				9	24	13	8	1	1			56	5.85	0.53
Fort Baker			5	7	1		8	2				23	5.72	0.91

TABLE 11
Lowest Frequency of All Syllable Types
(in kHz)

	1.75-	2.00-	2.25-	2.50-	2.75-	3.00-	3.25-	3.50-	3.75-	Total	Mean	SD
Tilden	2	25	19	4	4	79	34	1		168	2.79	0.46
Berkeley	3	46	33	7	15	111	74	38	4	331	2.88	0.50
Brooks Island			33	4	4	40	3	1		85	2.69	0.38
Richmond			2	1		3				6	2.67	0.38
Presidio		1	17	26	3	1				48	2.43	0.18
San Francisco		6	8	45	43	22	9	3	2	138	2.71	0.33
Lake Merced		6	9	57	43	6	1			122	2.58	0.22
Treasure Island		7	12	25	10	2	1	3		60	2.50	0.35
Fort Baker			1	5	12	10				28	2.78	0.21

TABLE 12

Summary of Tests Conducted between Population Pairs for 8 Variables of White-crown Songs

Population Pairs Tested	4[a]	5[a]	6[a]	7[a]	8[a]	9[a]	10[b]	11[b]	Total no. of differences
Berkeley-Tilden	$p<.005$	$p<.005$		$p<.005$	$p<.05$	$p<.005$		$p<.005$	6
Berkeley-Brooks Island	$p<.005$	$p<.005$	$p<.005$	$p<.005$	$p<.05$	$p<.05$	$p<.005$	$p<.005$	8
Presidio-Fort Baker			$p<.005$				$p<.005$	$p<.005$	3
Presidio-San Francisco			$p<.005$	$p<.05$					2
San Fransico-Lake Merced	$p<.005$	$p<.005$		$p<.005$	$p<.005$	$p<.005$	$p<.005$	$p<.005$	7
San Francisco-Treasure Island	$p<.01$	$p<.01$					$p<.005$	$p<.005$	4

[a] P values in columns 4 to 9 are for t-tests.
[b] P values in columns 10 and 11 are for x^2 tests.

Morphological Variation in Song
EAST SAN FRANCISCO BAY POPULATIONS
Distribution of White-crowns in Tilden Park and Berkeley

Marler and Tamura (1962) sampled the songs of White-crowns in the area around Inspiration Point in Tilden Park and in the City of Berkeley. Inspiration Point, "two miles to the northeast from the center of Berkeley," consists, as the authors point out, of open chaparral (fig. 1). In Berkeley, White-crowns found their niche in "town gardens and hedge rows."

Between 1968 and 1971, I recorded songs of White-crowns in Tilden Park and the cities of Berkeley, Albany, El Cerrito and Richmond. Songs recorded in Tilden Park will be referred to as Tilden themes throughout this study. Songs recorded in Berkeley, Albany, El Cerrito and Richmond will be known collectively as the Berkeley dialect. The map (fig. 1) reveals that the two song types are essentially allopatric in distribution, except for several localities in the Berkeley Hills, and in Strawberry Canyon to the northeast of the University of California campus.

Before describing song variation within these subpopulations, the allopatric geographical distribution of these two themes merits an explanation. The two shaded bands in figure 1 delineate the boundaries of Tilden Park and also indicate the general direction in which the two ridges run. The ridge along the eastern boundary of Tilden Park is known locally as San Pablo Ridge, the hills forming the western boundary of the park as the Berkeley Hills. I conducted two northwest to southeast transects, one along the crest of San Pablo Ridge and one along the crest of the Berkeley Hills. Three other transects were conducted: one from the City of Richmond to Brooks Island in San Francisco Bay, which will not concern us for the moment; and two west-to-east transects, one from the City of Albany to San Pablo Ridge, and one from the University of California campus in Berkeley, through Strawberry Canyon and the Berkeley Hills, to San Pablo Ridge.

White-crowned Sparrows are distributed in a series of clumps along my transect from Albany to the Berkeley Hills (fig. 1). They are absent from most of the park and appear again along the crest of San Pablo Ridge. There is a hiatus in distribution between the birds on the Berkeley Hills and those on San Pablo Ridge in Tilden Park along this transect, although habitat (disturbed chaparral) was available throughout this area. This break in the distribution of White-crowns is real. Fellow graduate students and hundreds of undergraduates have traversed that section of the park during field trips in connection with courses on the natural history of vertebrates; they found no resident White-crowns throughout the period of my study.

On the other hand, White-crowns are distributed in a continuous series of clumps from the Berkeley Hills, through the park to San Pablo Ridge. Between the two ridges a golf course has been built, lawns introduced, and park-like habitat created, similar to that encountered in parts of Berkeley. Man has provided suitable habitat in this section, permitting the occupancy of White-crowns.

The absence of White-crowns in much of the park between the two ridges merits an explanation. Hubbs (1918) pointed out that White-crowned Sparrows breed "in the humid region along the Pacific Coast." The subspecies *nuttalli* ranges from about Cape Mendocino (Mewaldt et al., 1968) to Point Conception in Santa Barbara County where the species range stops abruptly (Hubbs, 1918). Hubbs goes on to say that:

The cause of this sudden termination of the distribution of Nuttall's Sparrows is not hard to postulate, when we recall that the subspecies has the characters of birds frequenting humid regions. The outer coast of California is swept by moisture laden winds, causing fogs to form continuously during the summer on the hills. These winds blow hard across Conception almost uninterruptedly during the springs and summer months, but cease just around the Point, where the famous sunny climate of Santa Barbara is encountered, and where the range of *Zonotrichia leucophrys nuttalli* is abruptly terminated.

In the San Francisco Bay Area, White-crowns may be found "on the terrace between the hills of the San Francisco Peninsula and the sea" (Hubbs, 1918). Marshall (1948) found White-crowns "on the very wet facing slopes of the Richmond Hills." Thus the White-crowns of the East Bay are distributed along the crest and the windward side of the Berkeley Hills where the summer fog brings enough moisture for their subsistence. They are absent from the leeward side of the Berkeley Hills and the "valley" between the Berkeley Hills and San Pablo Ridge which are in fact "fog shadows" and probably too xeric for the species during the dry California summer. The golf course in Tilden Park, with its continuously watered greens, is therefore a man-made oasis for the species, and a possible "dispersal corridor" for birds hatched on the two ridges.

How can we explain the presence of White-crowns along the crest of San Pablo Ridge? O. P. Pearson (personal communication) pointed out that the needles of the pine trees that occur along the crest of the ridge trap some of the moisture laden fog coming from the west, and that the condensed moisture drips down under the trees and into the duff consisting of accumulated conifer needles. Even in the dryest part of the year, one can dig into the duff and find moisture. The combination of pine trees and duff catching the fog and making moisture a permanent factor along the crest of San Pablo Ridge probably permits the White-crowned Sparrow to exist there.

The allopatric distribution of the Berkeley and Tilden Park themes can thus be explained as follows. Before 1938, when the golf course was built, a xeric ecological barrier (the fog shadow) separated White-crowns living along the crest of San Pablo Ridge from those of the Berkeley Hills and Berkeley city. Dispersal of birds to and from these two ridges was probably rare, so that the White-crowns on San Pablo Ridge were isolated there long enough to evolve a distinctive song theme. The golf course provided a dispersal corridor, permitting birds singing either Tilden or Berkeley themes to come together in a zone of secondary contact in Strawberry Canyon where they exist sympatrically today. A few birds may have managed to cross the xeric barrier using other routes in Tilden Park west of the golf course, so that a few White-crowns singing Tilden themes exist alongside birds singing Berkeley motifs in other parts of the Berkeley Hills. It remains to be seen whether the status quo will be maintained, or if the Tilden themes will spread into the residential areas of Berkeley (or vice versa) to result in a "mosaic" distribution of the two currently allopatric regional themes.

Tilden Park Populations

MORPHOLOGICAL VARIATION IN SONG — Marler and Tamura (1962) described the songs of ten birds recorded near Inspiration Point in Tilden Park, Contra Costa County, California. These songs were all illustrated as beginning with a whistle, followed by a wide-banded buzz and finally a trill of simple syllable or W-B-SS. If the ten spectrograms illustrated in Marler and Tamura (1962:374) are examined, it may be seen that they are quite uniform in morphology. The introductory whistle in each song appears to consist of two or three short whistles, each one downward inflected and joined together by lighter areas. Because of amplitude modulation the first one or two whistles are apparent as three dark areas joined by lighter grey areas, which are in turn joined to a longer dark line which is also downward slurred. The second phrase in all cases is a wide-banded buzz, and as the authors have pointed out (page 374) the syllables in the terminal portion of the trill are the most reliable index separating the Inspiration Point songs from the Berkeley themes, being quite uniform throughout their samples.

In this study, slightly more variation was found with regard to the morphology of the introductory phrases (fig. 2). In songs A to C the introductory whistle consists of two downward inflected whistles joined together, and in songs E to G the introductory whistles are made up of three downward slurred whistles linked together. These match the songs illustrated in Marler and Tamura's (1962) paper. The introduction in song D (fig. 2) however consists of only one downward inflected whistle. This individual and its neighbor stood out from the rest of the birds in the population because of the distinct introductory whistle in their songs. Bird H sang themes with a prolonged introductory whistle consisting of two short and one long whistle joined together. Birds I to L had single introductory whistles, each one frequency modulated near the middle so that audio-spectrograms reveal a long slightly downward inflected black line with a trough near their centers.

Song M was recorded in the Berkeley Hills. The introductory whistle is typical of Tilden Park songs, however, the second phrase is a short buzz attached to a whistle, rather than the wide-banded vibrato of typical Tilden Park themes. Similar buzz-whistles have been described by Marler and Isaac (1961:203) as being present in the songs of Mexican Juncos *(Junco phaeonotus)*. They have hitherto not been found in the songs of White-crowned Sparrows. Song N has a shortened second phrase, a vibrato almost one-third the length of all the other buzzes (e.g., in Songs A to L) found in Tilden Park. I do not consider this phrase normal, however, because the bird appeared to be startled by my presence when it shortened the second buzz; the buzzes in all the rest of its songs recorded were of the normal length. I have records of other individuals apparently in conflict situations singing songs containing elements of "abnormal" length, or lengthened and irregular intervals of silence between the elements. These songs were never sustained in a bout.

Thus with larger samples than in the original study of Marler and Tamura (1962), I found slightly more variation with regard to the morphology of the introductory phrases in Tilden Park songs. However, as pointed out by Marler and Tamura all the song spectrograms taken together (fig. 2) reveal striking consistency with regard to the trill portion of the songs. Two birds resident in Tilden Park (Baptista, 1974) sang songs characteristic of the wintering populations of White-crowns belonging to the subspecies *pugetensis:* I have regarded these as exceptions rather than as the rule.

The Berkeley Populations

MORPHOLOGICAL VARIATION IN SONG – In its most typical form, the theme sung by populations of White-crowned Sparrows in Berkeley may be described as beginning with an introduction of two whistles followed by a trill of simple syllables or W-W-SS (Marler and Tamura, 1962; and fig. 3, A and B of present paper). A few birds recorded by Marler and Tamura (1962) sang songs with narrow banded vibrati constituting the second phrase (see, e.g., fig. 3, C of present paper), or W-B-SS. In no case did the authors find any Berkeley songs with a wide-banded vibrato as a second phrase. Additionally, the introductory whistle is usually morphologically less elaborate in the Berkeley than in the Tilden Park motifs. In the Tilden motifs the maximum frequencies of the terminal syllables is not too much lower than the highest frequencies of the syllables at the beginning of the trill (Marler and Tamura, 1962; and fig. 2, this study). In the audiospectrograms of songs recorded in the City of Berkeley, a noticeable drop in maximum frequencies between syllables at the beginning and at the terminal portions of the trills is evident so that to the trained ear the portion of the song that best separates the two regional themes is the terminal trill. The drop in maximum frequencies between syllables at the beginning and at the terminal portions of the trills in Berkeley themes enables the trained ear to hear it as if it were two trills, one following the other in rapid succession. The last syllable in each song terminates at a lower frequency than all the rest of the syllables in the trill (Marler and Tamura, 1962).

A number of minor variations from the more typical themes described above were encountered during the course of my study. Scattered throughout the population of White-crowns in Berkeley, were individuals singing songs containing a wide-banded buzz as the second phrase (see fig. 3D and E, and fig. 6). The frequency span of these buzzes varied from bird to bird. The wide-banded buzz is therefore not an element to be found only in Tilden themes, but occasionally also in songs recorded in Berkeley. Song F was recorded in Albany (see map, fig. 1) in 1970; the second phrase in this case is a buzz-whistle, described earlier in a Tilden Park motif (see fig. 2, M). A White-crown recorded on this same spot the previous year sang a song with two clear whistles in the introduction, suggesting that the bird singing song theme F was probably new to the area. In song G the second element appears to be a whistle superimposed with a buzz. There is a very special quality to this type of phrase, so that the trained ear may at once recognize it. Three other birds recorded in the Berkeley Hills also sang songs containing this phrase type. In song H the first syllable differs morphologically from all the rest in the trill in that it seems to have a short buzz attached. It was recorded both in 1969 and 1970 at the same locality in the Berkeley Hills, and so far has not been found elsewhere in Berkeley. Marler and Tamura (1962) have described syllables similar to this in their Sunset Beach sample. In song I (fig. 3), the first two syllables stand out from all the rest in the series in that each of these have an upward inflected "tail" attached. Songs J and K stand in sharp contrast from all the rest of the motifs recorded in Berkeley in that the introductory whistle is noticeably downward inflected, whereas introductory whistles in most Berkeley songs are usually only slightly downward slurred. The trained ear may catch these differences without any difficulty. Additionally, the first three syllables in songs J and K are more elaborate than the first syllables in other songs in Berkeley (e.g. songs A to G) in that each syllable is slurred gently and then steeply so that the picture on the audiospectrogram is of three syllables with "wings" as it were attached to the upper portions of each syllable. Three birds singing these songs were recorded in the same general area in 1969 and 1970. They have not been found as yet in any other localities within my transects. Songs L to N are a little more elaborate than more typical Berkeley themes in that the first introductory whistle in each song is more prolonged and is made up of two portions so that the unaided ear hears two whistles. It is difficult to ascertain from songs L and M whether the introductory phrase consists of one or two whistles. As Marler and Tamura (1962:370) have pointed out earlier, fluctuations in amplitude in various portions of a whistle are difficult to distinguish from "actual omission of some of the parts."

Looking now at songs illustrated in figure 4, motifs B to D1 differ from the more typical Berkeley themes in that the introductory whistle is frequency and amplitude modulated so that on the spectrogram one sees a whistle with three dark (loud) peaks and two light (soft) troughs. This has been described in an earlier paper (Baptista, 1972a) in which I also pointed out the close resemblance of the structure of this peculiar introductory whistle with similar whistles in songs of certain White-crowns raised in acoustical isolation by Marler and Tamura (1964; see also fig. 4, A2 and C2 in Marler, 1970a). Petrinovich (personal communication) has found similarly structured whistles in White-crowns that he and his associates raised in isolation chambers. In song C (fig. 4) the second phrase is once again a buzz-whistle, however the vibrato portion of the phrase is much shorter than the buzz portion in song F of figure 3 described earlier. Songs D and D1 are two motifs taken from a bout of one bird. In song D the maximum frequency of the first four syllables is noticeably higher than that in the rest of the syllables in the trill. However, in song D1 the ninth syllable in the trill is morphologically similar to the first four, the ninth syllable standing in sharp contrast with the four preceding and two following syllables in the second portion of the trill. I consider this a "mistake" in singing and not within the normal range of variation of songs recorded in this area. This "abnormal" ninth syllable was not sustained throughout the song bout recorded – the rest of the songs being almost identical to song D, with all the syllables in the second portion of the trill beginning at a lower maximum frequency than the first four syllables.

Hitherto all the variations described have been with regard to minor modifications of the morphology of the phrases or syllables found in the more typical Berkeley themes. A few birds varied from the more "normal" in that they sang songs with additions or deletions of entire phrases in the song. Themes A1 to A3, figure 4, were sung by the same bird. This individual occupied a territory on the northwestern edge of the University of California campus. Theme A1 is typical of the City of Berkeley, with two whistles in the introduction and a two-part trill, i.e. the eight syllables in the terminal portion of the trill have maximum frequencies lower than those in the first part. The last syllable terminates at a lower frequency than all the rest of the syllables in the trill, and in this respect also is typical of Berkeley. In songs A2 and A3, however, this bird added still another portion to the terminal trill, making it a three-parted trill. The maximum frequency of each syllable in the very last portion of the trill is higher than that in all the rest of the syllables. A2 and A3 were included in the illustrations to show that this same bird was also capable of varying the number of syllables preceding the terminal or third part of the trill – in A2 there are seven syllables preceding the terminal portion of the trill and in A3 there are eight of these elements. It is also noteworthy that in the "typical" Berkeley theme (A1) there are only eight syllables in the first portion of the trill which immediately follows the second introductory whistle. In other renditions of this same theme, this individual had nine syllables in this portion of the trill. In songs A2 and A3 there are nine syllables in the first portion of the three-part trill. It is noteworthy, then, that this individual was capable of varying the number of syllables in the first portion of the trill as well as the second part. In the earlier study by Marler and Tamura (1962) the only variation encountered within an individual's song bout was in the omission of syllables "from the last part of the trill," or in the lengths of the introductory whistles.

Marler and Tamura (1964) described a theme from Inverness, Marin County, California, with only a single whistle making up the introductory portion of the song. This was in contrast to themes from Inspiration Point, from Berkeley, and from Sunset Beach which in their samples seemed always to have two introductory phrases (Marler and Tamura, 1962, 1964). In my studies of song dialects, I recorded the songs of 22 individuals which exhibited only one introductory whistle in their songs (fig. 4, E to J). One was recorded about half a mile to the northwest of the University of California campus. The rest were in Albany, El Cerrito and Richmond. These were often neighbors of birds with the more usual two-whistled songs (e.g., in fig. 5). Songs H and H1 (fig. 4) are both from the repertoire of the same individual. In contrast to songs A to G, song H has two (instead of the more usual one) terminal syllables ending at a lower frequency than the others in the trill. In song H1, the penultimate syllable is downward inflected, then slurred upward, attaching itself to the upper portion of the last syllable. I do not consider the terminal flourishes in songs H and H1 as normal. They were never sustained in this individual's song bout, the rest of the songs recorded being of the type illustrated in songs E to G. They were included in the illustration to show that even when song is fully crystallized, an individual may occasionally make a "mistake" in singing. On the shores of Lake Merced in San Francisco, a mistake similar to that illustrated in H1 appears to have been "cystallized," that is, perpetuated by oral tradition and included as the penultimate element in the song dialect of that area (figs. 21 and 22; syllable type F in fig. 21). Song J in figure 4 not only lacks a second phrase, but concludes its song with an extra trill. The maximum frequency of each syllable in the terminal trill of song J is lower than that in all the other syllables in the preceding trill.

SUMMARY OF MORPHOLOGICAL VARIATION IN SONG THEMES CONSTITUTING THE BERKELEY DIALECT. – I found, as did Marler and Tamura (1962, 1964), that the dominant theme in this region may be described as having two introductory phrases and a single trill. The second phrase may be a whistle or a buzz, the two main themes are thus W-W-SS or W-B-SS. However, a few birds sang songs with only one introductory phrase or W-SS, and two birds sang songs with added trills at the ends, i.e., W-SS-SS and W-W-SS-SS. A few birds sang more than one song theme. Four individuals described earlier (Baptista, 1974) sang songs characteristic of flocks of the migratory form *pugetensis* wintering in the area; these are exceptions rather than the rule. The morphology of the syllables in the trill are the most reliable character identifying songs from the Berkeley population as reported by Marler and Tamura (1962).

Berkeley: Subdialects and Secondary Contact Areas

Song variants were not found randomly throughout the population but were usually clumped (see map, fig. 5). The picture that emerges is one of "subdialects" within a dialect area such as Nottebohm (1969b) has described for the Rufous-collared Sparrow *(Zonotrichia capensis)*. In areas where several song themes occurred sympatrically, a few birds sang two and one bird three of the motifs sung by other individuals within earshot (figs. 5 and 6).

Songs A1 to A3, figure 6, are three different motifs from the repertoire of an individual recorded at Arlington and Cutting Boulevards, Contra Costa County, California (map, fig. 5). The themes differ from each other with regard to the morphology of the first and second phrases and also in the details of the syllables in their trills. Songs B2 and B3 are from the repertoire of an individual recorded in Berkeley. They differ from each other in that the second phrase in B2 is a buzz and that in B3 this phrase is a pure whistle. There are also differences in the details of the syllables in the first portions of their trills. Song B1 was also sung by the same bird: It ended with the same "mistake" in singing described earlier (fig. 4, H1), a terminal element that was not sustained in its song bout. Songs C and C1 are from the repertoire of a third individual which occupied a territory neighboring bird A's, described above (map, fig. 5). Once again there are differences with regard to the morphology of the syllables in the trills as well as the introductory phrases of each song theme. However, in songs D and D1, (two themes from the repertoire of a fourth individual) the only difference between the two motifs is in the details of the second phrase, this being a pure whistle in song D and a buzz in song D1. Likewise in songs E and E1, two motifs from the repertoire of a fifth individual, no differences appear in the trills of each song. The two themes are distinguishable only with regard to the structure of the second phrase – this being a pure whistle in E and a buzz in E1. I should add that 10 or more sound spectrograms of each song theme illustrated in figure 6 were examined: Within these samples, except for the "abnormal" terminal flourishes discussed above, the only marked variation encountered between sound spectrograms of each song theme was in the number of syllables in the terminal portion of the trills and in the lengths of the introductory whistles from song to song.

In Strawberry Canyon (fig. 7 and 8), east of the University of California, Berkeley, campus, birds singing either the Berkeley or Tilden dialects occur sympatrically. In 1968, I recorded an individual that sang both themes (figs. 7 and 9). I did not record any other birds with bivalent repertoires at this locality during the three following years. It is possible that other birds in this area also had two song themes stored in their templates. However, since birds singing Tilden themes predominate here, it is possible that bivalent individuals are stimulated to match their neighbors with the dominant song in the canyon, so that Berkeley themes go unused. In 1969, I recorded two birds at the bottom of Strawberry Canyon singing Berkeley themes with two whistles in the introductions (figs. 7 and 10, A, B). One individual singing a Berkeley theme with a buzz as a second phrase occupied a territory directly below the Lawrence Hall of Science (figs. 7 and 10, C). Three individuals sang themes which I've interpreted as "cultural hybrids," including elements from both regional themes. Two motifs from one of these individuals are illustrated in fig. 9, B and C. Both these themes contain two pure whistles in their introductions, and in this respect match the "typical" Berkeley theme (fig. 9, A), rather than the Tilden motif (fig. 9, D). However, the syllables in the trills of B and C match the Tilden Park syllables of song D (fig. 9). Songs B and C were included in the illustration to show that this same individual could vary the song length by adding or omitting syllables toward the end of the trill as Marler and Tamura (1962) have discussed earlier. Another cultural hybrid recorded in 1969 is illustrated in figure 10, D. One finds a pure whistle typical of Berkeley city (see, e.g., songs in fig. 3), followed by a wide-banded vibrato, and finally a trill consisting of syllables with no marked variation in maximum frequencies, and therefore typical of Tilden (compare with song in fig. 10, K).

The theme recorded in figure 10, E was also recorded in Strawberry Canyon in 1969. The introduction consists of two downward inflected whistles joined together followed by a buzz, two characteristics of the Tilden themes. However, if the trill in this song is examined, one may see that there are more or less two sections to it: The terminal portions having maximum frequencies noticeably lower than the first part, a character of Berkeley themes. Song E may thus be regarded also as a cultural hybrid. Song F, a hybrid theme similar in many details to song E, was recorded in another part of the Berkeley Hills where Tilden and Berkeley themes occurred sympatrically. Two such themes were recorded in the golf course directly east of Strawberry Canyon, and four other such songs in secondary contact areas in the Berkeley Hills.

CHANGES IN THE COMPOSITION OF SONG THEMES RECORDED IN STRAWBERRY CANYON BETWEEN 1969 AND 1971. – Between 1969 and 1971 marked changes were recorded in Strawberry Canyon. Firstly, as may be seen in figure 8, no Berkeley motifs were recorded at the bottom of the canyon in 1971. Two Berkeley themes were recorded directly east of the Lawrence Hall of Science (fig. 8), both with buzzes in their introductions (see fig. 10, G to H1). Songs H and H1, both sung by the same individual, differ in the number of syllables in the first sections of their trills. The third Berkeley theme recorded directly below the Lawrence Hall of Science (figs. 8, 10J) had two whistles in the introductions. However, since the details of the syllables commencing its trills are noticeably different from the two-whistled songs recorded in 1969 (fig. 10, A and B), it would appear that this is a different individual. The "hybrid" motif (see fig. 10, I) recorded to the southeast of the Lawrence Hall in 1971 is also a new theme to the area. The first whistle in the introduction consists of two downward inflected portions joined together, typical of Tilden songs. However the second pure whistle is typical of Berkeley themes, and the trill that follows is two-parted if maximum frequencies of the syllables are considered, so that the trill is also more typical of Berkeley than of Tilden Park. This was the only theme of its kind that I recorded. The hybrid theme toward the middle of the canyon (see fig. 8 for location) could not be recorded as the bird would not sing continuous bouts for me. However it sounded identical to the songs recorded in 1969 and 1970 in this general area (see song D, fig. 10), and was very likely the same individual. The rest of the songs recorded in Strawberry Canyon in 1971 were typical of Tilden Park.

Thus, between 1969 and 1971, a number of changes have taken place with regard to the number and types of Berkeley and "hybrid" themes recorded in Strawberry Canyon. If the distribution of White-crowns in figures 7 and 8 are examined, it may also be seen that there were fewer White-crowns at the upper end of this study area in 1969. In 1971 (fig. 8) there is also a noticeable gap in the distribution of White-crowns beginning from the area where the southernmost "hybrid" song was recorded, to the cluster of Tilden themes northwest of the Botanical Gardens.

In the late summer of 1970, a grass fire swept through the area where the gap in White-crown distribution is evident in 1971. Although the grass returned in 1971, it is possible that the fire had altered the ecology of that particular area, in some way causing the birds to move out. Additionally, in 1971, workmen at some construction project were continually milling about the area directly above the Botanical Gardens, possibly disturbing the birds and causing them to leave. On the other hand, on the grounds around and directly east of the Lawrence Hall of Science, shrubs were planted in 1969. The nearby slopes were terraced and were originally intended to be built into car parks. However, the project was never finished: *Baccharis* and other shrubs have invaded providing new habitat for White-crowns, which have moved in. Strawberry Canyon, then, is an especially interesting locality, not only because two song dialects occur sympatrically, but also because it provides a readily accessible natural laboratory where one may study the effects of exposing naive White-crowns to several song themes in nature. In this short span of time I have demonstrated that new themes have emerged and old ones disappeared. It would be of extreme scientific interest to follow this population on an annual basis documenting possible future changes. One might ask, for instance, what the proportion of Tilden to Berkeley themes might become. Is one theme being selected for over the other? Would both dialects continue to survive through the years, or would they give way to a local subpopulation of White-crowns all singing hybrid themes of one kind of another?

Brooks Island Populations

MORPHOLOGICAL VARIATION IN SONG — Brooks Island in the San Francisco Bay is approximately 0.25 miles from Point Potrero in Richmond (fig. 12). The vegetation has been described by Lidicker and Anderson (1962) and consists of mostly soft chaparral. *Baccharis pilularis* is scattered over much of the island, providing cover and possible nesting sites for White-crowns. These emberizines were found throughout the island proper and also on the sand spit to the northwest on which *Baccharis* and other shrubs seem to have taken a firm hold.

Because of their remarkable powers of flight, one tends to regard most birds as being among the more mobile of vertebrates. Even to the sedentary form of the White-crowned Sparrow, the Richmond Harbor Channel should not prove too much of a physical barrier to dispersal, either to or from the island. The question that I asked, however, is that although they probably could disperse freely across the waterway, do they actually do so. If in times past the 0.25 miles of waterway has proved an effective barrier, "psychologically speaking," to the free movement of White-crowns, I should have found the population on the island singing a song theme or themes distinct from conspecifics on the Richmond mainland.

I visited the island on March 28, 1970 and again on June 7 and 8, 1971. On my 1970 visit my activities were confined to the northeast part of the island where I recorded the songs of 14 birds. In 1971 I recorded the songs of 28 birds throughout the island proper and also out on the sand spit toward the north (fig. 14). Four of these birds occupied territories from which songs were sampled the previous year. Their songs did not show any marked differences from those recorded in 1970. Since these 4 individuals may have been recorded the year before, only song spectrograms from the remaining 24 birds were merged with those from the 14 birds recorded the previous year when considering frequency and temporal aspects of variation for this island population. Data is thus presented on the songs of 38 individuals recorded on the island. No significant morphological differences were found between the samples for the two years.

The following descriptions refer to songs illustrated in figure 11. Song E is a motif typical of some of the birds in Berkeley and Richmond and may be used for comparison with songs recorded on the island. Song E is in fact a typical one-whistled Berkeley theme (compare with fig. 4). The syllables in the trill of song E are all simple in structure. As described earlier by Marler and Tamura (1962) the trill in Berkeley themes consists of two main types of syllables, differing slightly from each other in frequency span, so that the trained ear can recognize two trills, more or less, uttered sequentially in a very rapid tempo. Trills from the songs of Brooks Island birds are composed of both complex and simple syllables. Element D in figure 11 illustrates a simple syllable which may be found making up the last portion of all songs recorded on the island. Structurally it is slightly more elaborate than the syllables found in songs recorded from Berkeley. There appears to be a short vibrato attached to the upper part of the main portion of this syllable. Elements A to C are illustrations of three complex syllables recorded on the island. Each of these is made up of two "subsyllables" arranged in pairs, giving one the impression of two sounds uttered rapidly, one after the other. The second subsyllable in syllable C consists of a very short buzz attached to the very long downward inflected portion. The fifth complex syllable in song H illustrates a slight variation from the type C syllable in that the buzz attached to the second subsyllable is replaced by a single note. The structure of the first half of each complex syllable pair best distinguishes these three elements, being most complex in type A (i.e., containing the most number of notes), and least so in type C.

There are two main song themes on Brooks Island. Some birds sang songs with only one whistle in the introduction (fig. 11, F1 to K). Others sang songs with two whistles in the introductions (fig. 11, L to P). The first whistle in the two-whistled songs is much more elaborate than the second whistle, being amplitude modulated so that on the spectrogram one sees a spot followed by two dark lines then another spot. A closer examination will reveal lighter grey areas joining these darker spots, the lighter regions being frequency modulated to form three troughs. The two introductory whistles in these songs are followed by from three to four type C complex syllables, and finally one to five type D simple syllables. On June 8, 1971, one individual was heard singing a song with two introductory whistles followed by five complex syllables. Thereafter its songs contained only four complex syllables, the maximum number found in the other two-whistled songs recorded.

The one-whistled songs from Brooks Island (fig. 11, F1 to K) begin with a single whistle amplitude modulated in three areas. This whistle is followed by a trill of from three to five type A syllables, followed by a single type B syllable, and finally a trill of type D syllables. One individual's songs contained two type B syllables instead of the more usual one syllable (song K). Still another individual (see F1 and F2) could vary the number of type A syllables in each of its motifs, having from three to four in each song. Bird H would terminate some of its songs with a call note. This particular call appeared in 2 out of 13 motifs recorded, although I heard it in a few other songs which were not taped. It is morphologically similar to the "chup" call described by Marler (1970a: 3), who also described the songs of several isolates terminating with this element (see, e.g., fig. 5, A6, in Marler, 1970a: 10). I have found similar calls in the spectrograms of songs of two hand-raised White-crowns of the subspecies *pugetensis* (Baptista, unpublished).

Thus one-whistled songs differed from two-whistled songs not only in the morphology of the complex syllables, but also in that the trills of the former contained two types of complex syllables (types A and B, fig. 11) and the latter contained only one (type C). Both song types terminated with type D syllables. Within a song bout the individual may vary the number of terminal simple syllables. Only two birds, described earlier, varied the number of complex syllables as well, in successive renditions of their songs within a bout. The terminal simple syllable is the most consistent character appearing in all songs recorded on the island.

During the 1973 breeding season, McCollum (personal communication) heard a bird singing both one-whistled and two-whistled themes on the northeastern end of the island.

In 1971 I censused the number of singing White-crowns on Brooks Island, in an effort to determine the proportion of individuals singing one-whistled themes to those singing two-whistled songs. To my surprise the 42 birds singing one-whistled motifs were essentially concentrated on the western part of the island and the 26 individuals singing two-whistled songs occupied territories on the eastern end of the island (fig. 14). There appeared to be no physical or ecological barrier between the two groups of birds. The gaps in White-crown distribution shown in figure 14 indicate areas of open grassland and no cover for the birds. It remains to be seen whether in the years to come the two themes will continue to exist more or less geographically juxtaposed to one another. At least until the 1973 breeding season, the two song types remained allopatric in distribution (McCollum, personal communication).

Richmond Secondary Contact Zone

MORPHOLOGICAL VARIATION IN SONG. – In the vicinity of the warehouses and piers directly opposite Brooks Island (see map, fig. 12), I recorded the songs of five White-crowned Sparrows. One of these sang what I would call a Berkeley theme (fig. 13, A), three sang what I would categorize as Brooks Island motifs (e.g., songs D and E, fig. 13), and one bird sang a theme combining features of both song dialects (song C). Two other birds heard singing in nearby areas inaccessible to me sang Brooks Island themes.

Song B in figure 13 is a typical one-whistled Berkeley theme recorded in nearby Albany (see map in fig. 1) and may be used for comparison with the other songs illustrated in this same figure. If song B is compared with song A (recorded in Richmond) it may be seen that they are practically identical morphologically, except that bird A has added an extra low frequency rapid trill to the end of its song, a trill not present in song B. If songs D and E are compared with the motifs recorded on Brooks Island (fig. 11), it may be seen that the terminal simple syllables are identical to those found in songs recorded on the island (syllable type D, fig. 11). The complex syllables in songs D and E (fig. 13) are similar to the type C (fig. 11) complex syllables in Brooks Island themes. If songs D and E of figure 13 are compared with the two-whistled songs recorded on the island (fig. 11, L to P), it may be seen that the only difference between these is that the songs from the Richmond mainland lack a second phrase and may have a few more complex syllables than songs recorded on the island. This degree of individual variation may be found within any one of the mainland populations I've studied. I feel justified, therefore, in regarding songs D and E (fig. 13) as merely variants of the Brooks Island two-whistled themes.

If the first six simple syllables in song C (fig. 13) are compared with the first six simple syllables in song B, it may be seen that they are morphologically almost identical. The next six simple syllables in song C appear to have short buzzes attached to each one of them, and in this respect are morphologically similar to the first "subsyllable" of each complex syllable in songs D and E. It is possible that during song development bird C teased apart the two subsyllables of the complex syllables in Brooks Island songs, singing them at a different tempo. This is reminiscent of the comma-shaped terminal syllables found in songs recorded in the Presidio of San Francisco, which were sung either singularly or in pairs (see fig. 16) by different birds. The last two simple syllables in song C are identical to those in songs D and E. Thus the first six syllables in song C are typical of Berkeley themes, and the rest of the syllables are typical of Brooks Island, so that song C may be regarded as a "cultural hybrid."

It appears, therefore, that a population of White-crowns were isolated on Brooks Island long enough to evolve a distinct dialect, but because of population pressure have reinvaded the immediate mainland (fig. 12). On the Richmond waterfront, an area of "secondary contact," Berkeley and Brooks Island themes may now be recorded side by side with each other. Exposed to both these song types during the critical period when song learning takes place, one individual (fig. 13, bird C) has apparently improvised and constructed a song made up of syllables borrowed from both song dialects. It remains to be seen which of these song themes will continue to survive at this locality in the years to come. It would also be interesting to know if these themes would spread to the neighboring residential areas in the future.

WEST SAN FRANCISCO BAY POPULATIONS

City of San Francisco

DISTRIBUTION OF WHITE-CROWNS IN THE CITY OF SAN FRANCISCO – Figure 15 shows the distribution of sampling localities in the City of San Francisco. The inverted black triangles indicate spots where birds singing a song theme endemic to the northwest section of the Presidio were recorded — for purposes of description I will henceforth refer to these themes as the Presidio dialect. The open circles indicate localities where a very widespread song theme was recorded: These will be referred to as the San Francisco dialect. Finally, the black triangles to the south indicate localities where a theme endemic to the areas surrounding Lake Merced was recorded.

The stippled areas on the map indicate parks and golf courses. The unshaded areas are mostly residential areas. Birds singing the Presidio dialect occupied west facing slopes covered with moist chaparral, brushy areas at the edge of a golf course and gardens in residential areas for military personnel. Lake Merced is surrounded by slopes covered also by moist chaparral. Birds were found on these brushy slopes and also in grassy areas in the golf course where they were nesting in ornamental plants. Birds singing the San Francisco dialect were found in gardens in residential areas or in the various parks. Curiously, although habitat in terms of grassy areas for foraging and brush for cover and nesting sites were available in Stern Grove in San Francisco (see map, fig. 15), I found only one White-crown in this park. The Song Sparrow (*Melospiza melodia*) which is often sympatric with the White-crown in parks or in California chaparral was present in Stern Grove in some numbers.

MORPHOLOGICAL VARIATION IN SONG – In its most typical form, the City of San Francisco theme may be described as a whistle, followed by a buzz, then a trill of two complex syllables and a series of simple syllables, or W-B-CS-CS-SS (fig. 18, A to G and I to L). Five birds sang songs lacking a second phrase so that their songs may be written as W-CS-CS-SS (fig. 19, F and F1; fig. 20, H1 and H2). Bird H in figure 18 lacks one complex syllable, so that its description becomes W-B-CS-SS. However if the structures of the first two simple syllables following the one complex syllable are examined, one may see that they are slightly more elaborate than the next three simple syllables that follow in that the former seem to have a hint of a buzz attached to the upper ends. Morphologically, the first "subsyllable" of the single complex syllable in song H is quite similar to the first two simple syllables in this motif. It seems very likely that bird H has teased apart two subsyllables that normally make up one complex syllable, singing them at the same rhythm as the rest of the simple syllables in its songs. As discussed earlier, the commashaped syllables in the songs from the Presidio in San Francisco appear either singularly or in pairs (fig. 16), lending support to my view that during song development a few birds may "improvise" by changing the lengths of the intervals of silence between syllables within trills. Bird H appears to have done this. On scanning the songs illustrated in figures 18 to 20, one may find a great deal of variation with regard to the morphology of the buzzes sung. The buzzes may be of a very narrow frequency span (e.g., fig 18, I and K) or very wide-banded (fig. 18, F) with variations between these two extremes. The oscillation rates in these vibrati may be seen to vary from bird to bird also. In songs E and F (fig. 18) a very short buzz precedes the longer one which constitutes the bulk of the second phrase. Marler and Tamura (1962) have described two phrases similar to these two from Sunset Beach, Santa Cruz County, California (see, e.g., Marler and Tamura, 1962:371, fig. 2, O and P). Three birds (fig. 18, J; fig. 19, B and E) sang second phrases which appeared to be morphologically pure whistles superimposed with buzzes. Similar phrases have been described earlier in songs from Berkeley and Tilden Park. Pure whistles constituting the second phrase (e.g., fig. 18, M, O and P) are very local in distribution in San Francisco. Song M was one of three that I recorded on Telegraph Hill in downtown San Francisco. Songs O and P (fig. 18) are two of three birds that I recorded in the residential areas immediately north of Lake Merced. I found only one bird (not illustrated) singing a two-whistled song in the residential areas north of Golden Gate Park. A few birds were heard, but not recorded, singing two-whistled songs in Twin Peaks (map, fig. 15). Other than these, songs with a buzz constituting the second phrase in the introduction seem to be the most widespread song type throughout San Francisco. This is in contrast to Berkeley where two-whistled songs are widespread. Song H in figure 19, recorded in the residential areas north of Lake Merced has the whistle or buzz which usually constitutes the second phrase replaced by a short trill. For purposes of description I am calling this a staccato phrase. Each syllable in this phrase differs morphologically from syllables in staccato phrases recorded on Lake Merced (fig. 22), and appears to be mirror images of the "kip" note described by Marler (1970a:3). The two complex syllables in song H are also the only ones of their kind I've recorded.

On scanning the songs illustrated in figures 18 to 20 one may notice a great deal of individual variation with regard to the morphology of each complex syllable. Complex syllable types tend to be clumped in geographical distribution. For example nine birds were recorded on Union Square in downtown San Francisco (e.g., fig. 20, A to H2). The complex syllables in all their songs were morphologically quite similar. Figure 19, A to F1, illustrates motifs sung by six out of nine birds recorded in the vicinity of the California Academy of Sciences in Golden Gate Park (map, fig. 15). Songs A and A1 (figure 19) are two themes sung by the same bird. The complex syllable in song A was found in the songs of seven of these nine birds (see, e.g., fig. 19, B to E). The complex syllables in songs F and F1 of figure 19 are quite similar to those in song A, and appear to be a slight modification of the latter. The complex syllables in song A1 were found in the motifs of still another bird (not illustrated) in the vicinity. In morphology these syllables also appear to be slight modifications of the complex syllables in song A. In song A the complex syllable consists of four main notes, in song A1 there are only three main notes making up each complex syllable.

Still another example of clumped geographical distribution of complex syllable types is illustrated by the complex syllables in songs A and B of figure 18. These two songs were recorded in the Presidio; the complex syllables found in these themes were present in the songs of birds within the Presidio or in the nearby residential areas (see, e.g., fig. 18, E; see also figs. 16 and 17). The distribution of the complex syllable type in song C of figure 18 is worthy of comment. I found it in the songs of only two birds singing San Francisco themes. Song C was recorded in the Presidio. The complex syllable in song C was found in only one other "San Francisco" song, the second bird having been recorded on the San Francisco State College campus to the east of Lake Merced. However, complex syllables almost identical to those in song C were found in my entire sample of eleven birds recorded at Fort Baker, Marin County (fig. 24). It is also the most common syllable type to be found in songs recorded on the shores of Lake Merced (see songs in figs 21 and 22). Thus if motifs recorded in San Francisco were classed according to their complex syllable types and plotted out on a map, we would find a picture of clumped "cultural clones" of song themes — subdialects within the dialect area.

The feature that best distinguishes the San Francisco theme from Presidio or Lake Merced motifs is the terminal trill (fig. 18, A to M). Lake Merced themes also ended with buzzes or staccato phrases. The simple syllables in San Francisco themes are morphologically quite similar to those present in the trills of Berkeley and Tilden songs (see spectrograms in Marler and Tamura, 1962; and figs. 2, 3, 4, 6, present paper). The last syllable in each San Francisco theme usually terminates at a lower frequency than the other syllables in the trill; in this respect they are also similar to themes recorded in Berkeley and Tilden Park on the eastern portion of San Francisco Bay. A few birds sang songs with the last syllable terminating at a higher frequency than the others in the series (see song D in fig. 18).

Songs N to P in figure 18 are worthy of note because their terminal syllables differ morphologically from those found in the rest of the songs recorded in San Francisco. In song N a short buzz is attached to the upper portion of each of the last four syllables. In songs O and P a buzz is found only on the very last syllable. These three birds and a fourth individual that sang a song with these distinct syllables occupied territories within hearing of each other in the residential areas directly north of Lake Merced, once again illustrating a clumped distribution of a song variant.

Although the majority of the songs recorded in San Francisco terminate with a trill consisting of simple syllables, a few birds ended their songs with a coda, as it were, of from one to as many as seven complex syllables. Figure 19, A to f1 illustrate the songs of six birds recorded in the vicinity of the California Academy of Sciences in Golden Gate Park. Songs A and B are typically San Franciscan. In song C the terminal simple syllables in a more "typical" San Francisco theme are followed by a single complex syllable. Song D ends with three and song E ends with seven of these complex syllables. Songs F and F1 are two themes from the repertoire of one individual. These motifs lack a second phrase and end with two complex syllables. The two spectrograms were included in the illustration to show that this individual is capable of varying the number of simple syllables from song to song without changing the number of complex syllables at the beginning or the end of the trills — there are six simple syllables in song F and eight in song F1.

Figure 20, A to H1, illustrate eight out of nine birds recorded on Union Square in downtown San Francisco. There were an estimated twelve pairs of White-crowns on the square which was surrounded on all sides by about a half mile of skyscrapers and buildings from the next nearest resident conspecifics. Figure 20, I, illustrates a song from one of three birds I recorded on Telegraph Hill, the next nearest White-crowns I could find and record, and this song may be used for comparison with those on the square. Song I is typically San Franciscan with regard to sequencing of phrases and syllables, i.e., W-W-CS-CS-SS. The last two syllables have short buzzes attached to them and are reminiscent of those discussed earlier in songs N to P of figure 18. The songs recorded on the square have all the features found in typical San Francisco songs, but all end with a coda of from one (song E) to as many as four (song A) complex syllables. Morphologically these terminal syllables differ slightly from those in figure 19, discussed earlier, in that they appear to occupy a wider frequency span and are slightly longer in duration. Songs H1 and H2 are from the repertoire of an individual whose themes stand out from the rest of the Union Square motifs in that they lack a second phrase. Instead of the usual two complex syllables at the beginning of the trill (songs A to G), this individual's songs have four (song H2) to as many as five (song H1) of these complex syllables. A single song recorded from a second individual (not illustrated) countersinging with bird H also had only one introductory phrase, but had three instead of the more usual two complex syllables commencing the trill.

Summary of data on morphological variation in San Francisco songs: — The dominant theme may be described as a whistle, followed by a buzz, and then a trill of two complex syllables and finally a series of simple syllables (W-B-CS-CS-SS). There was a fair amount of variation with regard to the morphology of the complex syllables. A few birds had whistles as second phrases (W-W-CS-CS-SS). A few individuals lacked a second phrase in their songs (W-CS-CS-SS), and a few others ended their songs with terminal flourishes of from one to as many as seven complex syllables (W-CS-CS-SS-[CS] n; e.g., fig. 19). One bird sang two themes. The morphology of the simple syllables is the most consistent feature in San Francisco songs, however, a few exceptions were noted (e.g., fig. 18, N to P). Variants of any kind were usually clumped in distribution, giving one the impression of "subdialects" within this dialect area.

Presidio Populations

The song theme typical of the residential areas of San Francisco may be described as beginning with a whistle, followed by a buzz, then a trill of two complex elements, and finally a series of simple syllables. This may be written as W-B-CS-CS-SS. Two of these songs are illustrated in Figure 16S and Figure 17 A1 and may be used for comparison with motifs from the Presidio which are hereby described. Songs typical of birds from the northwest section of the Presidio (see map, fig. 15) are identical with those from adjacent residential areas in the City of San Francisco with regard to the sequence of elements that comprise the song, i.e. W-B-CS-CS-SS. The difference between the northwest Presidio themes and those of adjacent regions is that the terminal type 3 (fig. 17) syllables of the latter are replaced by the comma-shaped syllables (types 5 to 7, fig. 17).

There are also two main types of complex syllables in the population which are illustrated in figure 17 as types 1 and 2. Songs G to I in figure 16 are examples of themes with type 1 complex syllables and songs D to F with type 2 complex syllables. One bird (fig. 17, B1 and B2) sang a theme with a type 1 complex syllable, and a second theme containing a type 2 complex syllable. Still another bird (fig. 17) sang a Presidio (song A2) and a San Francisco (Song A1) theme.

There appears to be a certain amount of individual variation with regard to the morphology of the comma-shaped syllables as well, each individual tending to slur these in different ways. In songs J and K (fig. 16) these commas occupy a narrower frequency span than those in song G (fig. 16), and those in songs D to F (fig. 16) appear to be morphological intermediates between these two extremes.

Song S (fig. 16) represents a theme typical of the nearby residential areas in the City of San Francisco, the terminal syllables being of type 3 (fig. 17). If song S (fig. 16) is compared with songs R and Q, it may be seen that the latter two are morphological "hybrids" between the San Francisco and Northwest Presidio themes. In song R, six of the terminal syllables may be classed as type 3 (typical of San Francisco), and the very last one a "comma" characteristic of the Presidio. In song Q, four of the simple syllables are of type 3, and the last three are "commas" typical of the Presidio. Songs O and P are also "cultural hybrids" in that the terminal syllables are morphologically intermediate between type 3 and the comma syllables. This may be best appreciated if we look at songs C1 to C3 of figure 17, three motifs from a song bout of one individual. Song C1 is a cultural hybrid in that the last two simple syllables are commas, whereas the other four are San Francisco (fig. 17 type 3) syllables. Song C3 is also a cultural hybrid, but the third from the last syllable is a larger comma then the last two. If we examine the third from the last syllables of songs C1 to C3, it may be seen that in song C2 it is morphologically intermediate between that in songs C1 and C3, and almost identical to the syllables making up the terminal portion of the trills in songs O and P of figure 16. Gradual change in the form of a syllable in successive repetitions has been described for Cardinals (*Richmondena cardinalis*) by Lemon (1971), who has labelled the phenomenon "drift."

Songs L to N (fig. 16) represent other departures from the more typical Presidio theme (e.g., songs D to K). In song L a buzz is added to the terminal trill. This was the only individual which included a vibrato at the end of its trill so that its song really stood out from those sung by the rest of the population. It is noteworthy that although its song was abnormal for this area, it had mated successfully, and on June 1, 1969, this bird and its mate led me to their nest which contained four fully-feathered young probably very close to fledging. Songs M and N (fig. 16) represent another departure from the more "typical" Presidio theme in that the terminal commas are in pairs (type 8, fig. 17). The two complex syllables following the buzz in song M may be classed as type 1 (fig. 17) and the two complex syllables following the buzz in song N are of the type 2 variety. In all I recorded five birds with paired commas making up the terminal portions of their trill. These were all within hearing of each other in the north-easternmost part of my study area. Three other birds in the vicinity were in areas inaccessible to me, and could not be recorded.

INVASION OF THE PRESIDIO BY BIRDS FROM SAN FRANCISCO – If the distribution of my song samples in the Presidio are examined in the map (fig. 15), it may be seen that although the majority of the Presidio themes (black inverted triangles) are clustered in the area to the northwest, the adjacent "San Francisco city" themes (white circles) have, as it were, invaded the area, and may be found scattered through the population. My interpretation of this situation is that birds living in this section of the Presidio were once isolated from populations living in the more southern and eastern sections of San Francisco long enough to evolve a distinct theme. Because of man's activities and alteration of the habitat, dispersal corridors were created so that the two subpopulations were brought once again into contact with each other. The end result is that birds singing the San Francisco dialect were forced by population pressure and destruction of the habitat to disperse into the Northwest Presidio where the "hybrid swarm" of songs now exists. It is possible that in years to come even more changes may occur in the songs of birds living in this part of the Presidio.

Lake Merced Populations

As discussed earlier, the song characteristic of most of the City of San Francisco may be described as beginning with a whistle followed by a buzz, and ending with a trill of two complex syllables and a series of simple syllables (fig. 21, X), or W-B-CS-CS-SS. In contrast to this, the theme characteristic of the populations of White-crowns on the shores of Lake Merced and some of the surrounding residential areas begins with a whistle, followed by a buzz, and then a trill of from two to five (the more usual number being three) complex syllables, and ending with a buzz, i.e. W-B-CS-CS-CS-B (fig. 21, H to S). No simple syllables are present in these songs. These motifs may be best distinguished from San Francisco songs in that the Lake Merced themes, with only two exceptions, end with a type F syllable and a buzz (figs. 21 and 22). The two exceptions are: (1) a bird that ended its song with two complex syllables which followed the more usual terminal buzz W-B-CS-CS-CS-B-CS-CS (fig. 22, G); and (2) a bird that sang a song (not illustrated) with a trill of six complex syllables and no terminal buzz, i.e. W-B-CS-CS-CS-CS-CS-CS.

The complex syllables found in songs from the Lake Merced population are illustrated in figure 21, A to F. Syllable types A, D and E may also be found in San Francisco themes (see fig. 18, B, C and I). Types B and C (fig. 21) differ only slightly from types A and D, and are actually "cultural hybrids" of these two. The first "subsyllable" in syllable B is identical to the two subsyllables in D and the second subsyllable in B is identical with those in A. In syllable type C the same subsyllables found in type B are present but in reverse order.

Figure 21, H to M, illustrates songs in which the first two complex syllables are morphologically identical. Themes N to Q are themes in which the first two complex syllables are not alike. Except for song M, the second phrase in all the songs illustrated in figure 21 is a buzz. In song M it is a buzz-whistle, the only one of its kind I recorded in this population.

On the south shore of the more northern lake (map in fig. 15), nine birds sang songs with a short trill in place of the buzz which usually constitutes the second phrase (fig. 22, A2, B2, to G). For purposes of description I am calling these "staccato phrases" – they occupy the same position in the song as the more usual buzz phrase and are about the same duration as the latter. The number of syllables in each staccato phrase differs from bird to bird (fig. 22). Two birds recorded could vary the number of syllables in the staccato phrases from song to song in each bout of singing, e.g., songs C1 and C2 are both from the same bird. In C1 there are six syllables in the staccato phrase and in C2 there are seven. In song G, mentioned earlier, the terminal buzz phrase is followed by two complex syllables. The number of terminal complex syllables in G's repertoire varied from one to two, or they were left out altogether. It is noteworthy that although some of G's songs were abnormal for this area in that they end with a coda of two extra syllables, it was successful in securing a mate. This bird and its spouse led me to their nest containing two young Cowbirds and one White-crown nestling. The Lake Merced populations appear to be heavily parasitized by Brown-headed Cowbirds (Baptista, 1972b).

Songs H and I (fig. 22) also stand out in the population in that the staccato phrase constitutes the terminal flourish rather than the second phrase in the introduction. In song I there is only one terminal syllable. Bird H was capable of varying the number of terminal syllables in the staccato phrase, the number ranging from two to five from song to song. Although bird H's songs are abnormal for this area, it also managed to find a mate and breed successfully. This bird and its mate led me to their nest containing two nestlings about 5 to 6 days old on April 21, 1970.

Five birds on Lake Merced each sang two themes. Songs A1 and A2 in figure 22 were recorded from a bout from the same bird, and themes B1 and B2 were sung by still another individual. In A2 and B2 the second phrase is a staccato element. There are differences also with regard to the permutations and combinations of the various syllable types in these songs. As discussed earlier, birds with bivalent repertoires often matched songs sung by neighbors in bouts of counter-singing.

Besides singing more than one song theme, a few birds varied the number of complex syllables in each song within a song bout. Bird S in figure 21 could vary the number of type F complex syllables from two to three per song, to cite one example.

On the southeast shore of the more northern lake, I recorded three birds singing songs which I interpret as cultural hybrids between the typical Lake Merced and San Francisco themes. These are illustrated in figure 21, T to W. If these are compared with the San Francisco theme (song X, same figure), it may be seen that they all end with a buzz typical of Lake Merced, but are preceded by phrases and syllables typical of San Francisco in their morphology and sequencing. These may be written as W-B-CS-CS-SS-B. I heard at least two more of these themes in the residential areas to the east of the lake but could not locate the birds. Songs T and U (fig. 21) are two motifs sung by the same individual, illustrating that each bird singing "hybrid" themes may vary the number of simple syllables from song to song; there are two simple syllables in song T and three in song U.

Marler (1970a, fig. 5) illustrates sound spectrograms tracing the development of song of three White-crowned Sparrows raised in acoustical isolation. Bird C in figure 5 eventually sang a song ending with a trill made up of call notes described earlier in his paper as "Kip" notes (see Marler, 1970a, fig. 1C). The terminal trill in Marler's isolate song bears some resemblance to the staccato phrase recorded on Lake Merced (fig. 22, this study). It is tempting to speculate that the staccato phrase in the Lake Merced songs was derived from a series of ritualized Kip notes described by Marler (1970a). Further work on song ontogeny of a naive White-crown tutored with a Lake Merced staccato song is needed to substantiate this.

SUMMARY OF SONG VARIATION IN THE LAKE MERCED AREA. – The dominant theme on the shores of Lake Merced may be described as beginning with a whistle, followed by a buzz, then a trill of usually three complex syllables (sometimes two, four or five), and finally a terminal buzz, or W-B-CS-CS-CS-B. One individual had a buzz-whistle for a second phrase and nine individuals substituted the buzz normally constituting the second phrase with a staccato phrase. Five individuals sang two song themes each. One individual sang a theme with two extra complex syllables following the terminal buzz, or W-B-CS-CS-CS-B-CS-CS. Another individual sang a song with six complex syllables and no terminal buzz, or W-B-CS-CS-CS-CS-CS-CS. Three birds sang songs interpreted as "cultural hybrids" between San Francisco and Lake Merced themes, or W-B-CS-CS-SS-B.

The Treasure Island Populations

Treasure Island in the San Francisco Bay is occupied by a naval base situated about midway (3.5 miles) between Oakland and San Francisco. Hedgerows and lawns planted by the navy personnel provide ideal habitat for White-crowned Sparrows. On April 14, 1970, I recorded 7 birds from the south end of the island, and on July 12, 1971, I recorded 13 birds from the island's north end. The records for the two years were merged, for a total of 20 birds. Two other birds were heard singing on July 12, 1971, but these would stop singing every time I pointed my parabola at them so that I was unable to make recordings. Their songs did not appear to be any different from the dominant theme of the island.

MORPHOLOGICAL ASPECTS OF SONG VARIATIONS. – The descriptions that follow refer to songs and song elements illustrated in figure 23. The dominant song on the island may be described as beginning with two whistles, followed by a trill. The trill may be made up of two complex syllables (types P to V, fig. 23), followed by a series of simple syllables (types W, X), and terminating with a syllable at a lower frequency than the others (type Y). The impression one gets when hearing each complex syllable is two or three sounds uttered in rapid succession. The trills in songs A and B begin with three or four (type V) complex syllables, followed by a trill of type W syllables. Bird B was capable of varying the number of type V syllables from three to four, otherwise the only variation exhibited in successive renditions of songs by individual birds was in the length of the introductory whistle or in the number of types W or X syllables, such as Marler and Tamura (1962) have described for the three populations of White-crowns they studied.

The salient feature in the songs recorded on Treasure Island is the first whistle which is frequency modulated, slurring up, then down, and finally up again. The degree of slurring varies from bird to bird. This whistle is also amplitude modulated (see, e.g., fig. 23, O), so that on the spectrogram one may discern three black regions joined together by lighter grey areas. The impression one gets on hearing this is three discrete whistles delivered at different frequencies. Only one bird (bird G) lacked this whistle, the introduction in its songs consisting of only one whistle, reminiscent of the songs described by Marler and Tamura (1964) from Inverness in Marin County, California. Bird D's introductory whistle is hardly frequency modulated and is similar to the whistles recorded in Berkeley and Albany (see, e.g., fig. 3, L to N). Whereas the trills in the majority of the songs recorded began with two like complex syllables of types Q to V, song E contains only one complex syllable. The trill in song M begins with two unlike complex syllables (types P and Q).

The terminal portions of the trill seem to be the most uniform feature of the motifs recorded, being made up of syllable types W, X and Y. Thus, except for one bird which had only one whistle in its songs, the dominant song on Treasure Island may be described as beginning with two whistles followed by a trill of two (rarely one, three or four) complex syllables, and then a series of simple syllables. This may be written as W-W-CS-CS-SS.

If themes from Treasure Island are compared with songs recorded in San Francisco (figs. 18 and 23), it may be seen that the only real difference between motifs from these two localities is in the morphology of the first introductory whistle. This whistle in Treasure Island themes is more elaborate than those in San Francisco songs. Even this character is not consistent (see song D and G, fig. 23). The trills in the songs of both these localities are essentially identical. Based on the similarities of song morphology, it is my feeling that the birds on Treasure Island originated from San Francisco on the southern portion of the Bay rather than Berkeley and Oakland to the north where the song themes are quite distinct from the above (figs. 3 and 4).

Fort Baker, Marin County, Populations

Material from Fort Baker includes songs from two individuals recorded on April 5, 1969, and eight recorded on June 4, 1969. A single individual was recorded at nearby Fort Kronkite on July 21, 1969. Since its songs were morphologically similar to those recorded at Fort Baker, they were included in that sample which totalled eleven birds. The habitat at Fort Baker was coastal moist chaparral.

MORPHOLOGICAL ASPECTS OF SONG VARIATION. – Figure 24 illustrates the songs of 8 birds recorded at Fort Baker. All motifs recorded at Fort Baker may be described as beginning with a whistle followed by a syllable, then a buzz, and finally a trill made up of two complex elements followed by a series of simple syllables. This may be written as W-S-B-CS-CS-SS. The introductory whistles were morphologically similar in all the songs examined (fig. 24, A to H). The syllable that precedes each buzz however seems to exhibit some individual variability. In songs C and D it is inflected upward and then sharply downward. In song F it consists of three notes arranged close together. In the rest of the songs this syllable is more or less "comma" shaped, but slurred at different angles from bird to bird. The buzz in each song varies slightly in frequency span and oscillation rate for each individual also. The two complex syllables that follow are morphologically quite similar from song to song. The trill of simple syllables is also structurally quite similar throughout my sample. Songs A, B, and D terminate with a syllable which is slurred to a lower frequency than the rest in the series. Songs B and E terminate with syllables which are of a narrower frequency span than the other similar syllables. In songs C, G and H the songs terminate with two syllables which are slurred to a lower frequency than the others in the trill. The penultimate syllable in song H is inflected downward, then slurred upward. This penultimate syllable in song H is probably not normal, since it was never repeated. It is best regarded as a "mistake" in singing.

SUMMARY OF VARIATION IN FORT BAKER THEMES. – All the songs recorded may be described as beginning with a whistle, followed by a note-buzz, and then a trill of two complex syllables and a series of simple syllables, or W-S-B-CS-CS-SS. The last syllable may terminate at a frequency higher (e.g., song B) or lower (e.g., song A) than the rest of the syllables in the trill. A few songs (e.g., songs C and G) terminated with two syllables slurring to a lower frequency than the rest of the syllables in the trill. The morphology of the complex and simple syllables was quite similar in all the songs.

The role of the Golden Gate as a barrier to the dispersal of terrestrial vertebrates between Marin and San Francisco counties has been discussed by a number of authors including Miller (1941), Grinnell and Miller (1944), Hooper (1944), and Banks (1964). Two races of several avian species, e.g., the Oregon Junco *(Junco oreganus),* the Chestnut-backed Chickadee *(Parus rufescens)* and the Wrentit *(Chamaea fasciata),* "reach their limits at San

Francisco Bay" (Banks, 1964). Populations of White-crowns *(Zonotrichia leucophrys)* on each side of the Golden Gate have not differentiated enough morphologically to merit subspecific recognition (Banks, 1964). However, the differences in the morphology of songs between Fort Baker and the Presidio indicate that because of the channel, gene flow across the Golden Gate is probably rare.

Discussion and Conclusions

THE EVOLUTION OF SONG DIALECTS

Referring to song learning in birds, Thielcke (1970a) informs us that, "Tradition is the decisive barrier to a quick change in song. Even complete isolation does not lead to any changes if the tradition is not interrupted." Yet song dialects and subdialects exist. Under what natural conditions, then, could new song themes differentiate in populations of White-crowned sparrows, and indeed in any avian species exhibiting song dialects? Thielcke (1969:322) has pointed out that, "We have as yet no data explaining how mutually independent dialects arise within the same species or even within the same song." Herein are some speculations as to how White-crown song dialects or new song themes of any kind may evolve and some suggestions as to how these hypotheses may be tested experimentally in the laboratory.

The Role of Dispersal

Various authors (e.g., Marler and Tamura, 1962; Konishi, 1965; Thielcke, 1965a; Lemon, 1965; Armstrong, 1963; Payne, 1973) have pointed out that because juvenals of many avian species tend to settle near their place of birth, regional song themes tend to be local. Juvenile White-crowns probably disperse only short distances from their natal area. However, in areas where available habitat is limited and fragmented, a portion of each annual crop of juvenals must disperse greater distances. Especially in years when survival is high, population pressure would force most of these out of their natal demes. This would be adaptive with regard to the survival of the species, the long distance dispersers could function as "pioneers" seeking new habitat to colonize (Grinnell, 1922).

If these pioneers are isolated in time long enough from the "parent" population, new dialects or song themes may evolve. Johnston (1956, 1961) studied dispersal in juvenile Song Sparrows *(Melospiza melodia).* In that species, "The median distance of dispersal, hatch-site to breeding-site, for 34 Song Sparrows was 185 meters." However, he also found that, "nearly 10 per cent of the juveniles seem to have a tendency toward dispersal to relatively great distance." In other words, dispersal distance is skewed toward long distance in that species. This has been demonstrated in a few other birds and organisms (see review in Johnston, 1961).

We have no equivalent data for White-crowns as yet. However, Blanchard's (1941:33) data suggest that an occasional juvenal may disperse longer distances. She banded 58 nestlings and got 12 recoveries following dispersal from their parents' territories. One was shot, "at least a mile and a half from its birthplace," in the spring following the hatching year. The others were found on the University of California campus where they were born. Four bred on the campus within 200 to 525 yards from their parents' territories. One was collected nine months after its birth, "about 400 yards from its birthplace," "and would undoubtedly have bred." The six others were seen "one or more times, from a week to six months after fledging, all within 350 yards of where hatched." In summary, short distance dispersal would serve to preserve local song themes, but long distance dispersal, or dispersal away from the natal area would be a prerequisite to dialect development. The percentage of long distance dispersers in each White-crown population remains to be worked out.

The Role of Barriers

Just as geographic barriers are considered prerequisite to the evolution of new species (Mayr, 1963; cited by Thielcke, 1969), isolating barriers probably play an important role in the differentiation of new song dialects. Some data have emerged from this study of song dialects of White-crowns. I suggested that the White-crowns on San Pablo Ridge, Tilden Park, were probably historically separated by an ecological barrier, a belt of xeric habitat, which resulted in the differentiation of distinct song themes to be found today in each of these subpopulations. An ecological barrier of uninhabitable young stands of conifers was postulated by Thielcke (1965a, 1969) as separating Short-toed Tree Creepers *(Certhia brachydactyla)* in Spain from those of neighboring European countries: The Spanish birds have evolved distinct song themes in isolation.

The role of water barriers isolating populations of Chaffinches (*Fringilla coelebs*) on the Azores Islands was demonstrated by Marler and Boatman (1951) and more recently by Knecht and Scheer (1968), who have described Chaffinch dialects on the islands distinct from the mainland of Europe. Similarly, the White-crowns on Treasure and Brooks islands are separated from mainland populations by the waters of the Bay. The Golden Gate appears to be an effective water barrier to free dispersal of White-crowns, the populations on each side of the Gate singing distinct song dialects.

The birds on Union Square in downtown San Francisco sing a distinct theme (fig. 20), having been isolated on the square by a "sea" of buildings all around. Armstrong (1963), citing Sick (1939), relates a similar situation with Chaffinches in Stuttgart where distinct Chaffinch rain call dialects exist in three city parks. In one case, two dialects "were sharply divided by a railway line and a few blocks of houses." In another case, "the boundary went right through a region densely populated with Chaffinches, and there was a mixed zone with pure calls of both forms as well as transitions between the two forms" (Thielcke, 1969).

Thielcke (1969:312) has called attention to the existence of "compact" and "extremely fragmented" avian populations. City populations of White-crowned Sparrows are "fragmented" in distribution. One may travel several blocks without encountering any of these birds. Each group of White-crowns, acoustically isolated from other such groups by blocks of houses, could easily evolve minor deviations from the main themes, forming "subdialects" as I have demonstrated for the birds in the San Francisco Bay Area (see, e.g., fig. 5 and fig. 20). A detailed study of song dialects of White-crowned Sparrows in a less fragmented habitat, such as some of the California coastal chaparral is in progress.

In the transect from the Presidio to Lake Merced in San Francisco I described three dialects in a continuum, one replacing the other over distance as Payne (1973) has described for dialects of viduines (*Vidua* spp.). This is not to say that historically barriers of some kind did not exist separating neighbouring White-crown dialects in San Francisco from each other.

The Accumulation of Cultural Micromutations in Song

In each dialect area, I have described a main theme with a number of minor deviations from the norm. These deviations involved: (1) alterations of syllablic structure; (2) changes in the morphology of phrases, e.g., replacement of whistles by buzzes or staccato phrases; (3) deletions of phrases or syllables, e.g., one-whistled songs appearing in populations singing predominantly two-whistle songs, or the presence of only one complex syllable instead of the more usual two in a San Francisco theme (fig. 18, H); (4) additions of extra phrases or syllables (see figs. 4, A2 and A3; and 16, L); (5) reordering of the sequence of elements, e.g., the Lake Merced themes with the staccato phrase at the end instead of at the beginning of each song (fig. 22, H); (6) changes in the rhythm of the trill, e.g., the Presidio songs with the comma-shaped syllables sung in pairs instead of as spaced single syllables (fig. 16, M, N); (7) the ritualization of call notes and their inclusion in songs, e.g., the staccato phrase in Lake Merced themes (fig. 22) apparently composed of alarm calls, and the Brooks Island theme (fig. 11, H) with a ritualized "chup" call. Can these changes take place, if tradition is not interrupted? Data from studies on song ontogeny of the White-crown discussed below, suggest some plasticity in the learning process.

Errors in Learning

In an earlier paper (Baptista, 1972a) I described the songs of a House Finch (*Carpodacus mexicanus*) that included elements of a White-crown's songs in its own. One explanation proposed for this "mistake" in learning was that individual differences exist in the learning abilities of these finches. The same remarks may apply to the White-crowned Sparrow. Marler (1960:362) discussed song learning in birds, pointing out that, "from the studies so far carried out, it appears that the copying of another's song is never quite precise, so that learning may also facilitate the development of individual characteristics."

Marler (1970a:13) also exposed two naive White-crowned Sparrows to a White-crown and a Song Sparrow (*Melospiza melodia*) training song from day 50 to day 71 of age. One individual sang an isolate theme (Marler 1970a, fig. 10, A4). The song developed by the second bird bore no resemblance to the training song with regard to syllable morphology; however, a whistle and a trill portion could be distinguished, suggesting, as Marler (1970a) pointed out, that some learning of the White-crown training song may have taken place.

Since the results obtained for each of Marler's (1970a:13) two experimentals were not the same, it is possible that members of natural populations may likewise exhibit differences with regard to learning abilities. Some birds may make "mistakes," so to speak, so that minor alterations of syllabic structure may be manifestations of "learning errors." "Errors in learning" were postulated by Lemon (1965) to explain new elements occurring in the songs of Cardinals (*Richmondena cardinalis*), and by Payne (1973) for Viduine Finches (*Vidua* spp.).

In a more recent paper, Lemon (1971) interpreted the apparent variability of song learning abilities of Cardinals as a "positive process" rather than a negative one which the word "error" implies. This view would suggest that differences in song copying abilities of birds are in fact manifestations of variability with regard to individual dispositions to improvise. This may be manifested as "drift, or gradual alteration in the form of a syllable in successive repetitions, through invention of new syllables, and through recombination of new syllables" (Harris and Lemon, 1972). Either interpretation could explain the minor alterations of syllable morphology often encountered in song learning experiments. Evidence of drift was shown in the songs of one individual recorded in the Presidio of San Francisco (fig. 17, C1 to C3).

Improvisation

Marler (1970a:fig. 9) tutored a naive White-crown from day 35 to day 56 with a theme recorded at Inverness. The training song may be described as a whistle, followed by a trill of two complex syllables, and then a series of simple syllables and a terminal buzz, or W-CS-CS-SS-B. This individual finally sang a fair copy of the training song, containing three instead of two complex syllables, or W-CS-CS-CS-SS (see Marler 1970a: fig. 9, A3). A bird captured in the field at about 35 days of age and raised in a sound-proof box developed a similar song (Marler 1970a: fig. 4, E5). (Two other such themes are illustrated in Marler, 1970a: fig. 8.) These data may be interpreted as "inventiveness" on the part of some individuals, which may account for some members of natural populations adding or deleting certain syllable types as discussed earlier.

More examples of improvisation by White-crowns were given by Marler and Tamura (1964; Marler, 1970a) who illustrated sound spectrograms of isolate songs containing "ritualized call notes." A few birds on the shores of Lake Merced and a bird on Brooks Island may have behaved likewise (figs. 11, H and 22).

Improvisation in terms of borrowing syllables from different training songs and constructing "hybrid" themes has not yet been demonstrated in the laboratory. However, I have shown from field studies that this may sometimes occur in nature. A few birds learned themes from visiting migrants of the race *pugetensis,* one individual even constructing a theme combining trills from both the migrant and resident races (Baptista 1974). It is possible, therefore, that an occasional *nuttalli* may improvise by including only single syllables or phrases from themes sung by visiting migrants into their own songs. The terminal buzz in the one theme recorded at the Presidio in San Francisco (fig. 16, L) may have been of this origin. Similarly the extra terminal trills in the songs of two birds recorded in Berkeley and Richmond (fig. 4; fig. 13, A) may have been learned from migrants. They are reminiscent of the "slow trill" described by De Wolfe et al. (1974) for songs of White-crowns belonging to the subspecies *gambelii.*

The Role of Inadequate Instruction

Thielcke (1965a, 1965b, 1969, 1970a, 1970b) studied song development in two European species of Tree Creepers (*Certhia* spp.). In those species calls developed from begging notes, and begging notes were later ritualized (through learning) in fixed sequences as species and population specific songs. With Kaspar Hauser experiments, it was determined that the correct sequence of calls in each song had to be learned. Immelmann (1969) studied song development in Zebra Finches (*Poephila guttata*). In that species the morphology of song elements was learned first, and the correct sequence next. We have no comparable data for White-crowned Sparrows. However, like Zebra Finches, if White-crowns learn the correct structures of syllables first, and the sequence in which they are to appear in the song next, an individual with an inadequate amount of instruction, in terms of the correct *amount* of exposure to the training song, may sing a theme with the syllables and phrases in a different order from that in the training motif. This may explain the origin of the two themes recorded on Lake Merced (fig. 22, H, I) with the staccato phrase at the end of the song instead of in the introduction. There may be a critical amount of exposure to a training song required, a "critical dose" if you will, before the experimental may sing a theme with the correct syllablic structures as well as the correct sequence of elements as in the training song. If a brood of White-crowns is bereft of a father because of a predator or some other cause, and if no other White-crowns are singing in the near vicinity, these juveniles may grow up with an "incorrect amount" of exposure to the art of White-crown singing. Such individuals may eventually sing themes with modified syllabic structures or the correct syllables in different sequences. In such an impoverished acoustic environment these same individuals may even be stimulated to "improvise" and incorporate call notes or other elements into their songs. Indeed, it was only in the acoustically impoverished environment of a Kasper Hauser box that Marler and Tamura (1964; also Marler, 1970a) found birds incorporating call notes into their crystallized songs.

The Role of Countersinging

Marler's (1956, 1960) remarks regarding the role of countersinging in preserving local Chaffinch dialects may apply also to the White crowned Sparrow.

ON WHITE-CROWN DIALECTS AND PANMIXIA

Data on song variation in sedentary populations of the White-crowned Sparrow are similar to those for the Rufous-collared Sparrow studied by Nottebohm (1969b) and King (1972) in that each White-crown dialect area may be broken up into a number of "subdialect" regions. Brooks Island, the most adequately sampled locality, was the most dramatic example of this phenomenon for the White-crown (fig. 14). In the Aquita populations Nottebohm (1969b) found at least two "subdialects" (see also Nottebohm, 1969b, figs. 4 and 8). On the other hand, dialects of sedentary populations of the White-crowned Sparrow appear to be more local in distribution than those of the Rufous-collared Sparrow. Nottebohm (1969b) found that for the latter species, dialects remained unchanged over "hundreds of miles of homogenous habitat" (Nottebohm and Selander, 1972).

Nottebohm's (1969b; see also King, 1972) subdialects are distinguished solely on the basis of the introductory portions of the songs. In contrast, a few groups of White-crowns, e.g., on Union Square in San Francisco city, sing songs with additional syllables appearing after the terminal trills (fig. 19). Based on these added elements small subdialect groups may also be recognized.

Song learning in the White-crowned Sparrow terminates before dispersal from the natal area (see introduction). Because of the local distribution of song dialects, Marler and Tamura (1962), Konishi (1965) and Nottebohm (1970) have suggested therefore that some inbreeding must occur within populations of this sparrow singing a common theme. Because the subdialects are likewise clumped in distribution, it would follow that gene flow is probably also restricted between subdialect groups. Panmixia in a population of White-crowns is probably never achieved in one generation. In Miller's (1947) words, panmixia is probably "graded in space and in time." Similarly, Nottebohm (1969b:313), studying populations of *Zonotrichia capensis*, proposed that gene flow was probably restricted at the boundaries of subdialect as well as dialect groups. King (1972:348) also studying song dialects of *Zonotrichia capensis* reported that "geographic variation in song themes was accompanied by variation in body size." Nottebohm and Selander (1972), using the technique of starch gel electrophoresis in studying populational variation in proteins, found a clinal gradient across three dialects of *capensis* at three loci. This, the authors added, could be attributed to distances separating these populations, to restricted gene flow between them, an altitudinal gradient in selective forces, or an interaction between the last two factors (Nottebohm and Selander, 1972:142).

Deviation from panmixia has also been suggested for populations of Wren-tits (*Chamaea fasciata*) (Miller, 1947), Song Sparrows (*Melospiza melodia*) (Miller, 1947; Johnston, 1956, 1961), House Mice (*Mus musculus*) (Selander, 1970a, 1970b) and Viduine Finches (*Vidua* spp.) (Payne, 1973). Payne (1973) proposed that his picture of the distribution of viduine song dialects pointed to a population structure of a series of intergrading "neighborhoods" predicted in the "Isolation by Distance" model of Wright (1932, 1943, 1950). The Wright model, as interpreted by Miller (1947), proposed that: "a group of many moderately small, imperfectly isolated populations is the most favorable situation for developing new combinations of genes with, occasionally, new and perhaps high selective values; these combinations, because of their advantage, and with or without changing environmental conditions, may then take over larger areas, supplanting part or all of the former loosely connected group of populations." Fragmentation of the gene pool, or graded panmixia, not only between White-crown dialects but also within a dialect area (from one end of a dialect area to another, as suggested by the clumped distribution of themes) would be adaptive according to the above theory. That deviation from panmixia is adaptive has been suggested by authors dealing with all the vertebrate species discussed above.

It is very likely that natural populations of many species of animals may be shown to fit the Wright model. However, gathering this data by means other than the dialect study approach (serviceable only if vocalizations are learned prior to dispersal) generally involves many years of "capture-recapture analysis of individuals" in a population, or "biochemical studies of protein polymorphisms" which entails the destruction of individuals (Payne, 1973). To this I might add that since animals are not destroyed in song-dialect studies, the investigator is allowed to follow possible changes in population structure through time.

Payne (1973) pointed out that dialects also permit us to distinguish between "island" models and "continuum" structures, and other possible population systems. Both continuum and island models appear to be represented in the populations of White-crowned Sparrows in the San Francisco Bay Area. The three dialects across the San Francisco Peninsula occur in a continuum with one replacing the other over distance. The subdialects are all geographically juxtaposed, pointing also to a continuum structure. Ecological islands and real islands also have been described (see section on barriers). Finally, song distribution points to possible recent changes in population structure of these sparrows, e.g.: (1) the invasion of the Presidio by birds from San Francisco city; (2) the golf course reuniting the Tilden Park and Berkeley populations; (3) the changes that occurred in Strawberry Canyon with regard to the presence of new Berkeley themes in the space of three years, pointing to the arrival and establishment of recent immigrants from the city; (4) the invasion of the mainland by birds from Brooks Island.

THE POSSIBLE FUNCTION OF DIALECTS

Andrew (1962:586) was of the opinion that: "The selective advantage of dialects is still obscure, and it may well be that song learning has evolved purely as a simple means of insuring the transmission of complex species-specific song, and that the existence of dialects is a functionless by-product." Thielcke (1969:322) proposed that: "The function of dialects is perhaps to reduce variability in order to increase the effectiveness of the signal."

Marler and Tamura (1962), on the other hand, have suggested that: (1) Dialects may promote philopatry; that is, young birds may be attracted to breed in areas where conspecifics sing the song they themselves had learned in their youth. (2) A female's choice of mate may be affected by songs heard during her youth. This, they suggested, "may have repercussions upon the genetic constitution of the population."

Konishi (1965) showed that female White-crowns also learn the local dialects. Milligan and Verner (1971) presented evidence indicating that White-crowned Sparrows react more strongly to their own dialect than to a foreign one. Nottebohm (1969b, 1970) studied song variation in the congeneric *Zonotrichia capensis,* and found that each dialect was associated with a different habitat. Building on data from the above studies on White-crowns, Nottebohm (1969b) has suggested that: (1) Dialects promote both philopatry and positive assortative mating; that is, females select as mates males that sing their own dialects. (2) Inbreeding of this kind is advantageous in serving to preserve gene pools that adapt birds to local conditions. In this respect his conclusions are similar to those of Konishi (1965:781). (3) Nottebohm (1969b:314; see also King, 1972) proposed further that assortative mating "may be instrumental in the emergence of step clines. . . ." More recently Nottebohm and Selander (1972:142; see also Nottebohm, 1972) have proposed that avian dialects "may well discourage the saltatory dispersal of genes. . ." and "may reduce gene flow between populations to rates such as we may find in many land mammals. . . ."

Earlier, I presented data indicating that White-crowned Sparrows singing more than one subdialect tended to match themes played on a tape recorder or sung by neighbors. This would suggest that individuals may distinguish between subdialects as well as dialects. Although Nottebohm (1969b:313) suggested that gene flow may be restricted between subdialect as well as dialect boundaries, he does not mention the possibility of subdialects likewise promoting Ortstreue or some inbreeding. This idea should also be considered, especially in view of the fact that Milligan and Verner's (1971) material on dialect recognition is regarded as in support of the assortative mating theory.

If song themes, dialects, and subdialects, function in promoting some inbreeding in sections of populations, then it would be of adaptive significance that most birds in the population sing only one theme. However, it could also be adaptive for a few birds in the population to sing more than one song type. This could increase their chances of finding mates: They could pair with females selected from either of two neighboring dialect (or subdialect) singing populations (or subpopulations). This would facilitate some gene flow between subpopulations, and assist in maintaining a "graded" panmixia. Some pairing between birds singing different themes undoubtedly occurs (see below). Birds singing more than one theme may be a double insurance that this occurs more frequently.

However, whereas the clumped distribution of song themes, subdialects as well as dialects, suggest that juveniles do not wander far from their birthplace, it has yet to be shown that these vocalizations are instrumental in promoting this phenomenon. Habitat imprinting may occur independently of imprinting to a song dialect. Löhrl (1959) studied dispersal in the migratory Collared Flycatcher (*Ficedula albicollis*). He showed that hand-raised juveniles, released during a "critical period," when they presumably learned features of the locality of release, returned the following year to breed. Von Haartman and Löhrl (1950) found the song of this flycatcher to be extremely variable and gave no evidence for the existence of dialects.

Two song dialects of the Rufous-collared Sparrow from two different life zones were found to grade into each other (Nottebohm and Selander, 1972:142). The authors have proposed that: "Female choice of mate probably includes birds deviating a little toward either end of the dialect gradient." Birds singing atypical songs from the Presidio and Lake Merced (this study) were shown to breed successfully. Earlier (Baptista 1973, 1974) I presented evidence that several sedentary White-crowned Sparrows that had learned song themes from wintering migrants belonging to the subspecies *pugetensis* paired with local *nuttalli* females. Indeed, two females injected with testosterone sang *nuttalli* themes. Moreover, one of these pairs nested successfully, two young being found in their nest. With the White-crowned Sparrow at least, females may sometimes choose males that sing songs deviating more than a little from the local dialect. This is not to say that a tendency for females to choose mates singing their own themes eventually may not be shown statistically.

The hypotheses that dialects promote philopatry and/or positive assortative mating, if proven, would demonstrate a mechanism effecting partial genetic isolation between dialect populations or segments of populations. Experimental verification, however, is still lacking.

Summary

Song variation in sedentary populations of the White-crowned Sparrow (*Zonotrichia leucophrys nuttalli*) was studied in the San Francisco Bay Area of California. Based on an analysis of over 2400 song spectrograms of over 400 birds, it was found that there is not one song theme in each area, but a dominant motif or "dialect" with a number of minor variations or "cultural micromutations" in song.

Song variants were not found randomly throughout the populations but were clumped in distribution forming a number of subdialect areas within each dialect region.

Although most individuals sang only one theme each, a few individuals sang from two to four themes. A few birds were apparently "misimprinted" with songs sung by wintering migrants belonging to the subspecies *pugetensis*. One individual sang two *nuttalli* themes, one *pugetensis* theme, and a song combining syllables from the songs of both races (Baptista, 1974).

Birds from the City of Berkeley are separated from those of San Pablo Ridge in Tilden Park by a xeric belt uninhabitable to White-crowns. A Tilden Park theme has thus evolved in isolation. In a few localities in the Berkeley Hills the two dialects occur sympatrically; in these areas of "secondary contact" two "parental" dialects, an occasional "cultural hybrid" (i.e., songs combining features of both regional themes), and one "bilingual" bird that sang both dialects, were found.

Birds on Brooks Island 0.25 miles from the Richmond mainland sing two distinct themes or "subdialects" which are geographically juxtaposed. Birds singing one of the island themes apparently have reinvaded the immediate mainland where Brooks Island and Berkeley themes occur sympatrically. A "cultural hybrid" was found at this locality.

Birds on Treasure Island in the San Francisco Bay sing songs which differ only slightly from those of the City of San Francisco about 3.5 miles across the waters of the Bay. Based on the similarities of song morphology, the White-crowns on Treasure Island probably originated from populations in San Francisco.

Three dialects occur in a continuum on the San Francisco Peninsula, from the Presidio to Lake Merced, with no apparent geographical barriers separating them. There are narrow areas of sympatry where San Francisco and Lake Merced themes occur sympatrically. Several "cultural" hybrids were found. The San Francisco theme seems to have invaded the Presidio, perhaps due to disturbance of the original habitat by man, so that the two dialects occur in mosaic fashion in the Presidio. Three birds singing "cultural hybrid" themes were found, and one individual was "bilingual."

Data on song variation and geographical distribution of song themes in the White-crowned Sparrow and other species enables one to propose theories whereby song dialects may evolve: these theories were presented.

Since no apparent barriers separated the three San Francisco dialects, and no barriers were found between subdialect regions (e.g., on Brooks Island, or El Cerrito), it was suggested that birds singing these themes are separated only by distance, resulting from the tendency of individuals of these species to settle near their place of birth. The mosaic distribution of subdialect groups and dialects in a continuum point to a population structure of genetically semi-isolated neighborhoods predicted in the Isolation by Distance model of Wright. The possible functions and adaptive significance of song dialects were discussed.

Literature Cited

ANDREW, R. J.
    1962. Evolution of intelligence and vocal mimicking. Science, 137:585-589.

ARMSTRONG, E. A.
    1963. A study of bird song. Oxford University Press, London.

BANKS, R. C.
    1964. Geographic variation in the White-crowned Sparrow *Zonotrichia leucophrys*. Univ. Calif. Publ. Zool., 70:1-123.

BAPTISTA, L. F.
    1972a. Wild house finch sings White-crowned Sparrow song. Z. Tierpsychol., 30:266-270.
    1972b. Cowbird parasitism on the White-crowned Sparrow and Wrentit in the San Francisco Bay Area. Auk, 89:879-882.
    1972c. Demes, dispersion and song dialects in sedentary populations of the White-crowned Sparrow (*Zonotrichia leucophrys nuttalli*). Ph.D. dissertation, University of California, Berkeley.
    1973. Der Einfluss der Gesänge der Zugvogelrasse *pugetensis* auf die Gesangsentwicklung der Standvogelrasse des Weisskopfammerfinken (*Zonotrichia leucophrys nuttalli*). *In:* D-OG Jahresversammlung (1972) in Saarbrücken. J. Ornith., 114:379-380.
    1974. The effects of songs of wintering White-crowned Sparrows on song development in sedentary populations of the species. Z. Tierpsychol., 34:147-171.

BLANCHARD, B. D.
    1936. Continuity of behavior in the Nuttall White-crowned Sparrow. Condor, 38:145-150.
    1941. The White-crowned Sparrows (*Zonotrichia leucophrys*) of the Pacific seaboard: Environment and annual cycle. Univ. Calif. Publ. Zool., 46:1-178.
    1942. Migration in Pacific Coast White-crowned Sparrows. Auk, 59:47-63.

BLANCHARD, B. D., and M. M. ERICKSON
    1949. The cycle in the Gambel Sparrow. Univ. Calif. Publ. Zool., 47:255-318.

BORROR, D. J.
    1960. The analysis of animal sounds. *In:* W. E. Lanyon and W. N. Tavolga (eds.), Animal sounds and communication: 26-37. American Institute of Biological Sciences, Washington, D. C.
    1961. Songs of finches (Fringillidae) of Eastern North America. The Ohio Journal of Science, 61:161-174.

BORROR, D. J., and W. W. H. GUNN
    1965. Variation in White-throated Sparrow songs. Auk, 82:26-47.

CORTOPASSI, A. J., and L. R. MEWALDT
    1965. The circumannual distribution of White-crowned Sparrows. Bird-Banding, 36:141-169.

DAVIS, J.
    1958. Singing behavior and the gonad cycle of the Rufous-sided Towhee. Condor, 60:308-336.

DE WOLFE, B. B.
    1968. Nuttall's White-crowned Sparrow. *In:* A. C. Bent and Collaborators,' Life histories of North American Cardinals, Grosbeaks, Buntings, Towhees, Finches, Sparrows, and Allies, Part three. U. S. National Museum Bulletin, 237.

DE WOLFE, B. B., D. D. KASKA, and L. J. PEYTON
  1974. Prominent variations in the songs of Gambel's White-crowned Sparrows. Bird-Banding, 45:224-252.
DIXON, K. L.
  1969. Patterns of singing in a population of the Plain Titmouse. Condor, 71:94-101.
FALLS, J. B.
  1969. Functions of territorial song in the White-throated Sparrow. *In:* R. A. Hinde (ed.), Bird vocalizations: 207-232. Cambridge University Press, Cambridge.
GRINNELL, J.
  1922. The role of the "accidental." Auk, 38:373-380.
GRINNELL, J., and A. H. MILLER
  1944. The distribution of the birds of California. Pac.Coast Avif., 27:1-608.
HARRIS, M. A., and R. E. LEMON
  1972. Songs of song sparrows (*Melospiza melodia*); individual variation and dialects. Can. J. Zool., 50:301-309.
HECKENLIVELY, D. B.
  1970. Song in a population of Black-throated Sparrows. Condor, 72:24-37.
HINDE, R. A.
  1958. Alternative motor patterns in chaffinch song. Anim. Behav., 6:211-218.
HOOPER, E. T.
  1944. San Francisco Bay as a factor influencing speciation in rodents. Misc. Publ. Mus. Zool. Univ. Mich., 59.
HUBBS, C. L.
  1918. The distribution of Nuttall's Sparrow in California. Auk, 35:321-326.
IMMELMANN, K.
  1969. Song development in the Zebra Finch and other estrildid finches. *In:* R. A. Hinde (ed.), Bird vocalizations: 61-74. Cambridge University Press, Cambridge.
JOHNSTON, R. F.
  1956. Population structure in salt marsh Song Sparrows. Part 1. Environment and annual cycle. Condor, 58:24-44.
  1961. Population movements of birds. Condor, 63:386-389.
KERN, M. D., and J. R. KING
  1972. Testosterone-induced singing in female White-crowned Sparrows. Condor, 74:204-209.
KING, J. R.
  1972. Variation in the song of the Rufous-collared Sparrow, *Zonotrichia capensis*, in Northwestern Argentina. Z. Tierpsychol., 30:344-374.
KNECHT, S., and U. SCHEER
  1968. Lautäusserung and Verhalten des Azoren-Buchfinken (*Fringilla coelebs moreletti* Pucheran). Z. Tierpsychol., 25:155-169.
KONISHI, M.
  1964. Song variation in a population of Oregon Juncos. Condor, 66:423-436.
  1965. The role of auditory feedback in the control of vocalization in the White-crowned Sparrow. Z. Tierpsychol., 22:770-783.
  1969. Time resolution by single auditory neurones in birds. Nature, 222:566-567.
KROODSMA, D. E.
  1971. Song variations and singing behavior in the Rufous-sided Towhee, *Pipilo erythrophthalmus oreganus*. Condor, 73:303-308.
LEMON, R. E.
  1965. The song repertoire of cardinals (*Richmondena cardinalis*) at London, Ontario. Can. J. Zool., 43:559-562.

1967. The response of cardinals to songs of different dialects. Anim. Behav., 15:538-545.
1968. Coordinated singing by Black-crested Titmice. Can. J. Zool., 46:1163-1167.
1971. Differentiation of song dialects in Cardinals. Ibis, 133:373-377.

LIDICKER, W. Z., JR., and P. K. ANDERSON
1962. Colonization of an island by *Microtus californicus*, analysed on the basis of runway transects. J. Anim. Ecol., 31:503-517.

LÖHRL, H.
1959. Zur Frage des Zeitpunktes einer Prägung auf die Heimatregion beim Halsbandschnäpper (*Ficedula albicollis*). J. Ornith. 100:132-140.

MARLER, P.
1956. Behaviour of the Chaffinch (*Fringilla coelebs*). Behaviour, Suppl., 5:1-184.
1960. Bird songs and mate selection. *In:* W. E. Lanyon and W. N. Tavolga (eds.), Animals sounds and communication: 348-367. American Institute of Biological Sciences, Washington, D. C.
1967a. Comparative study of song development in sparrows. Proc XIV Intern. Ornithol. Congr.: 231-244.
1967b. Acoustical influences in birdsong development. The Rockefeller University Review, Sept.-Oct.: 8-13.
1970a. A comparative approach to vocal learning: song development in White-crowned Sparrows. J. Comp. Physiol. Psychol., Monograph. 71, 2.
1970b. Birdsong and speech development: Could there be parallels? Amer. Sci., 58:669-673.

MARLER, P., and D. J. BOATMAN
1951. Observations on the birds of Pico, Azores. Ibis, 93:90-99.

MARLER, P., and W. J. HAMILTON III
1966. Mechanisms of animal behavior. Wiley, New York.

MARLER, P., and D. ISAAC
1960. Physical analysis of a simple bird song as exemplified by the chipping sparrow. Condor, 62:124-135.
1961. Song variation in a population of Mexican juncos. Wilson Bull., 73:193-206.

MARLER, P., and M. TAMURA
1962. Song "dialects" in three populations of White-crowned Sparrows. Condor, 64:368-377.
1964. Culturally transmitted patterns of vocal behavior in sparrows. Science, 146: 1483-1486.

MARSHALL, J. T., JR.
1948. Ecologic races of Song Sparrows in the San Francisco Bay Region. Part I. Habitat and abundance. Condor, 50:193-215.

MAYR, E.
1963. Animal species and evolution. Harvard University Press, Cambridge, Massachusetts.

MEWALDT, L. R., S. S. KIBBY, and M. L. MORTON
1968. Comparative biology of Pacific Coastal White-crowned Sparrows. Condor, 70:14-30.

MILLER, A. H.
1941. Speciation in the avian genus *Junco*. Univ. Calif. Publ. Zool., 44:173-434.
1947. Panmixia and population size with reference to birds. Evolution 1:186-190.

MILLER, A. H., and V. D. MILLER
 1968. The behavioral ecology and breeding biology of the Andean Sparrow, *Zonotrichia capensis*. Caldasia 10:83-154.
MILLIGAN, M. M., and J. VERNER
 1971. Inter-populational song dialect discrimination in the White-crowned Sparrow. Condor, 73:208-213.
MULLIGAN, J. A.
 1963. A description of Song Sparrow song based on instrumental analysis, Proc. XIII Intern. Ornithol. Congr.: 272-284.
 1966. Singing behavior and its development in the Song Sparrow *Melospiza melodia*. Univ. Calif. Publ. Zool., 81:1-76.
NICE, M. M.
 1941. The role of territory in bird life. Amer. Midl. Naturalist, 26:441-487.
 1943. Studies in the life history of the song sparrow. 2. The behavior of the Song Sparrow and other Passerines. Trans. Linn. Soc. New York, 6:1-329.
NOTTEBOHM, F.
 1969a. The "critical period" for song learning. Ibis, 111:386-387.
 1969b. The song of the chingolo, *Zonotrichia capensis*, in Argentina: description and evaluation of a system of dialects. Condor, 71:299-315.
 1970. Ontogeny of bird song. Science, 167:950-956.
 1972. The origins of vocal learning. The Amer. Nat., 106:116-140.
NOTTEBOHM, F., and R. K. SELANDER
 1972. Vocal dialects and gene frequences in the Chingolo Sparrow (*Zonotrichia capensis*). Condor, 74:137-143.
PAYNE, R. B.
 1973. Behavior, mimetic songs and song dialects, and relationships in the parasitic indigo birds (*Vidua*) of Africa. Ornithological Monographs, 11.
PEYTON, L. J., and B. B. DE WOLFE
 1968. A distinctive song pattern in Gambel's White-crowned Sparrow. Condor, 70:385-386.
PETERSON, R. T.
 1941. A field guide to western birds. Houghton Mifflin, Boston.
RICE, J. O'H., and W. L. THOMPSON
 1968. Song development in the Indigo Bunting. Anim. Behav., 16:462-469.
ROBERTS, J. B.
 1969. Vocalizations of the Rufous-sided Towhee, *Pipilo erythrophthalmus oreganus*. Condor, 71:257-266.
SELANDER, R. K.
 1970a. Behavior and genetic variation in natural populations. Am. Zool., 10:53-66.
 1970b. Biochemical polymorphism in mice. *In:* R. J. Berry and H. N. Southern (eds.), Variation in mammalian populations. Zool. Soc. of London Symposia, 26.
SICK, H.
 1939. Über die Dialektbildung beim Regenruf des Buchfinken. J. Ornith., 87:568-592.
SKUTCH, A. F.
 1954. Life histories of Central American birds. Pac. Coast Avif., 31.
THIELCKE, G.
 1965a. Gesangsgeographische Variation des Gartenbaumläufers (*Certhia brachydactyla*)

im Hinblick auf das Artbildungsproblem. Z. Tierpsychol., 22:542-566.
1965b. Die Ontogenese der Bettlelaute von Garten und Waldbaumläufer (*Certhia brachydactyla* Brehm und *C. familiaris* L.) Zool. Anz., 174: 237-241.
1969. Geographic variation in bird vocalizations. *In:* R. A. Hinde (ed.), Bird vocalizations: 311-339. Cambridge University Press, Cambridge.
1970a. Lernen von Gesang als möglicher Schrittmacher der Evolution. Z. zool. Syst. Evolutionsforsch, 8:309-320.
1970b. Vogelstimmen. Springer-Verlag, Berlin.

THOMPSON, W. L.
1968. The songs of five species of *Passerina*. Behaviour, 31:261-287.

THORPE, W. H.
1958. The learning of song patterns by birds, with special reference to the song of the Chaffinch (*Fingilla coelebs*). Ibis, 100:535-570.
1964. *In:* A. L. Thomson (ed.), A new dictionary of birds. Singing: 739-750.

THORPE, W. H., and P. M. PILCHER
1958. The nature and characteristics of sub-song. British Birds, 51:509-514.

VERNER, J., and M. M. MILLIGAN
1971. Responses of male White-crowned Sparrows to playback of recorded songs. Condor, 73:56-64.

VON HAARTMAN, L., and H. LÖHRL
1950. Die Lautäusserungen des Trauer- und Halsbandfliegenschnäppers, *Muscicapa h. hypoleuca* (Pall.) und *M. a. albicollis* Temminck. Ornis. Fenn., 27:85-97.

WRIGHT, S.
1932. The role of mutation, inbreeding, crossbreeding and selection in evolution. Proc. 6th Int. Cong. Genetics, 1:356-366.
1943. Isolation by distance. Genetics, 28:114-138.
1950. Genetical structure of populations. Nature, 166:247.

PLATES

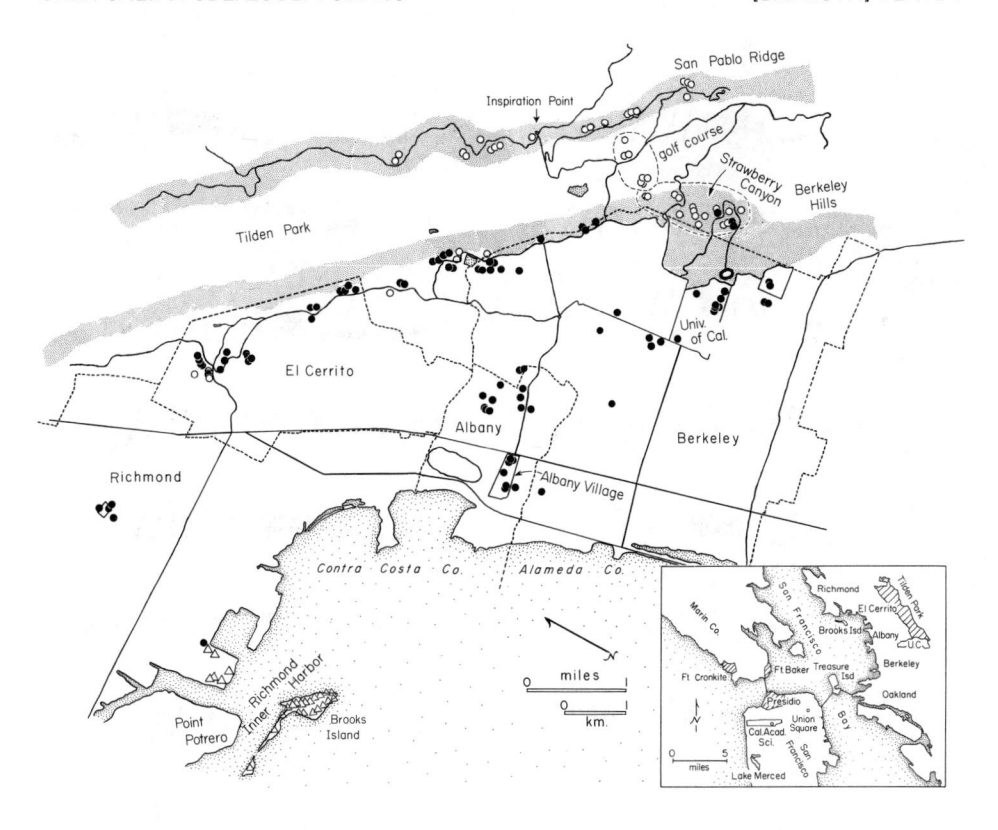

Figure 1. Map showing localities in East San Francisco Bay where song samples were recorded. Tilden themes are indicated by open circles, Berkeley themes by dots, and Brooks Island themes by open triangles. The two shaded areas show approximately the eastern and western boundaries of Tilden Park. They also indicate the direction in which two ridges run — San Pablo Ridge to the east of the park and the Berkeley Hills to the west.

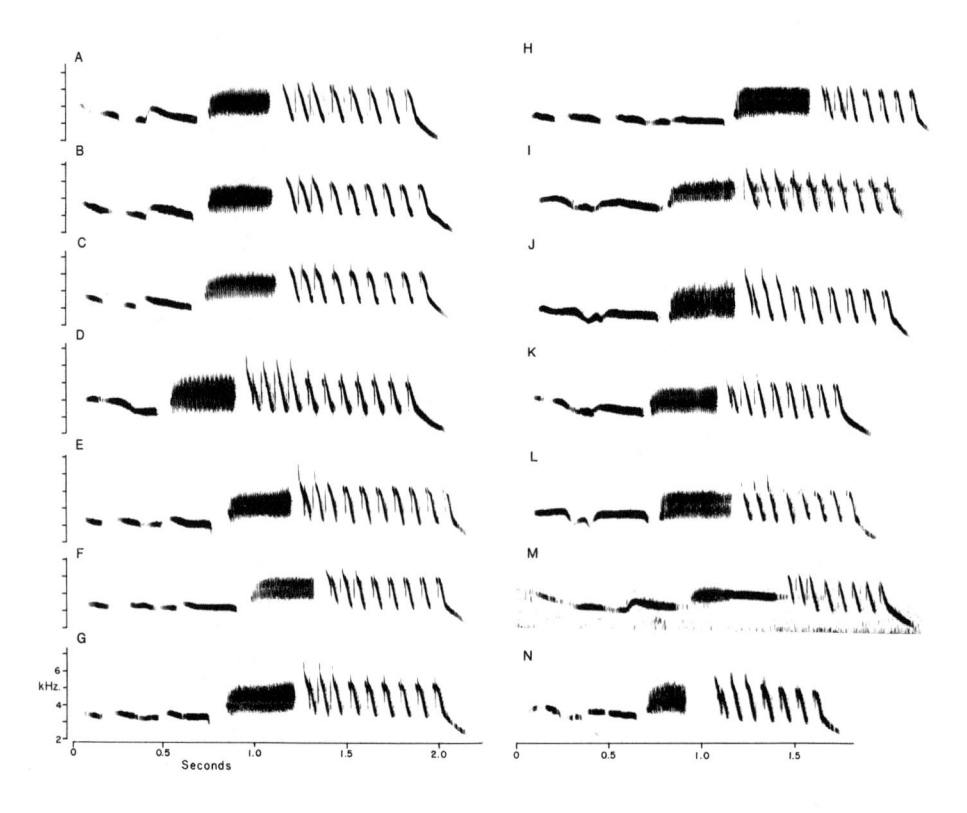

Figure 2. A to L are song spectrograms recorded in Tilden Park. Song M was recorded in the Berkeley Hills; note that the second phrase is a buzz-whistle. The second phrase in song N, also recorded in Tilden Park, is shortened.

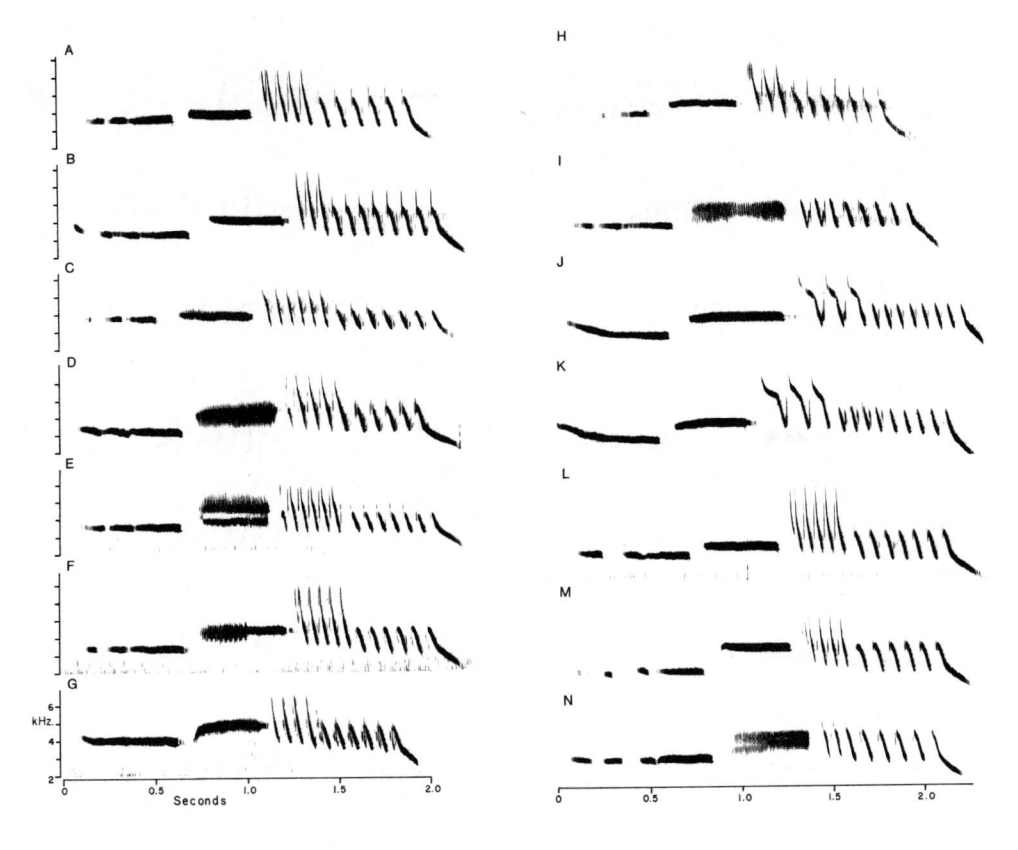

Figure 3. Songs A to N represent samples from Berkeley and adjacent cities. See text for fuller explanation of figure.

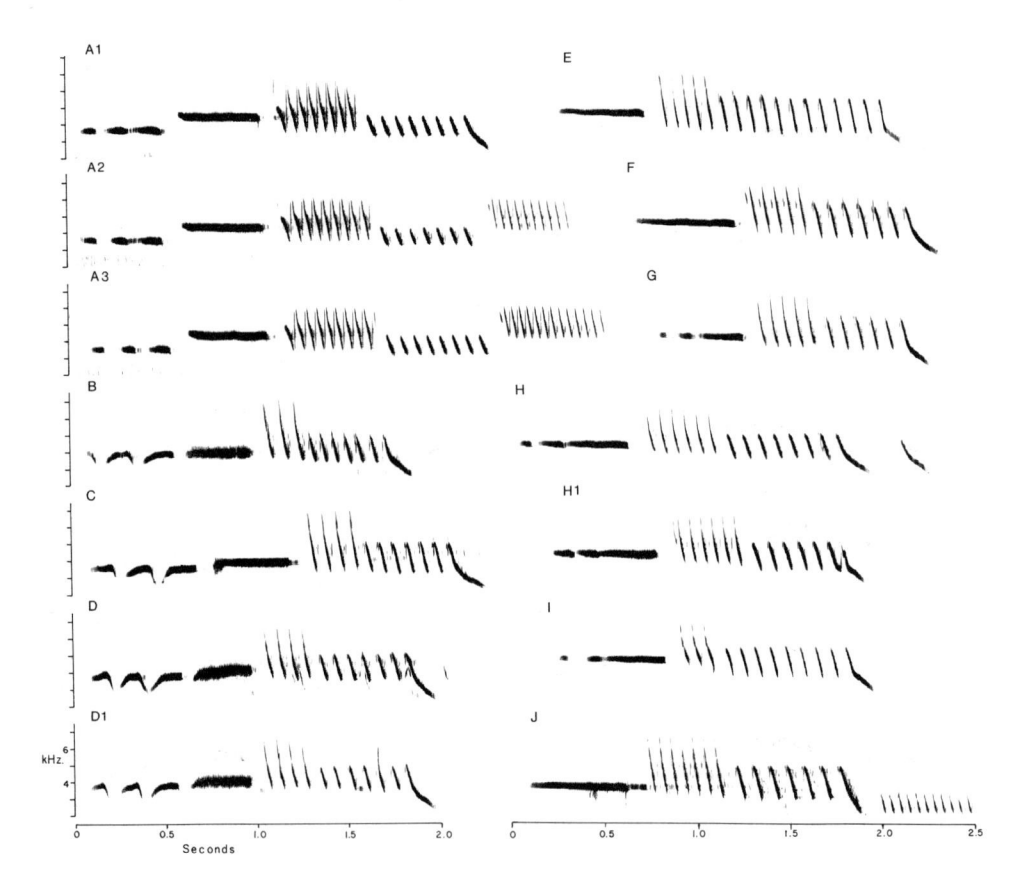

Figure 4. Songs recorded in Berkeley and neighboring cities. Song A1 is a typical Berkeley theme. Themes A2 and A3 (both sung by the same bird that sang A1) each have an extra terminal trill. Songs B to D1 have frequency modulated introductory whistles reminiscent of whistles in songs of isolates (see text). Themes E to J lack a second phrase. Bird J has also added a terminal trill to its song.

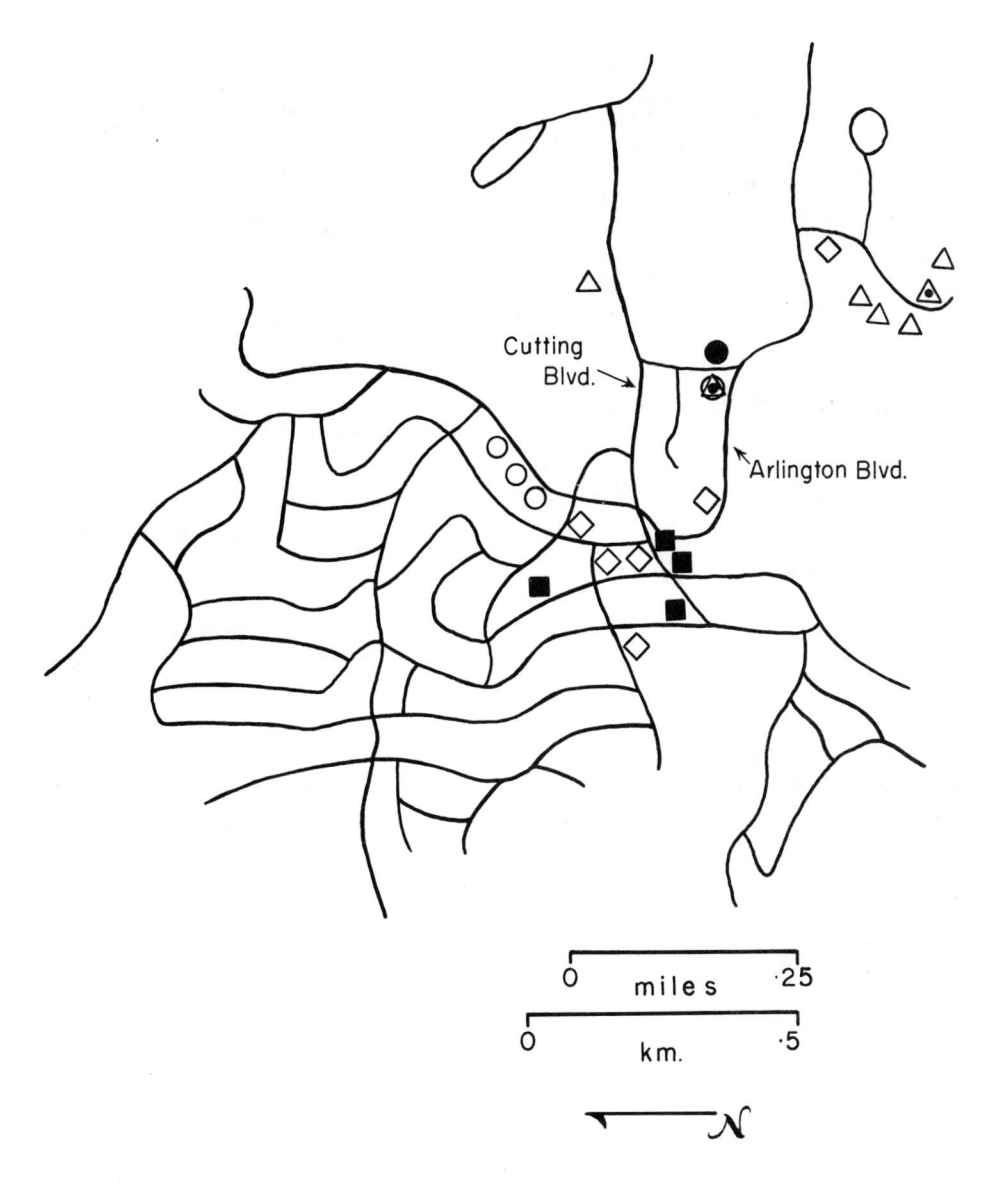

Figure 5. Map showing distribution of song themes at Arlington and Cutting Boulevards in El Cerrito, California. Clear circles are two-whistled songs, black circles indicate songs with a buzz as the second phrase, black squares are Tilden themes, clear triangles are songs with frequency modulated whistles (see also fig. 6). The clear triangle superimposed with a black spot indicates a bird with a bivalent repertoire, and the circle superimposed with a clear triangle and a black spot indicates a trivalent individual.

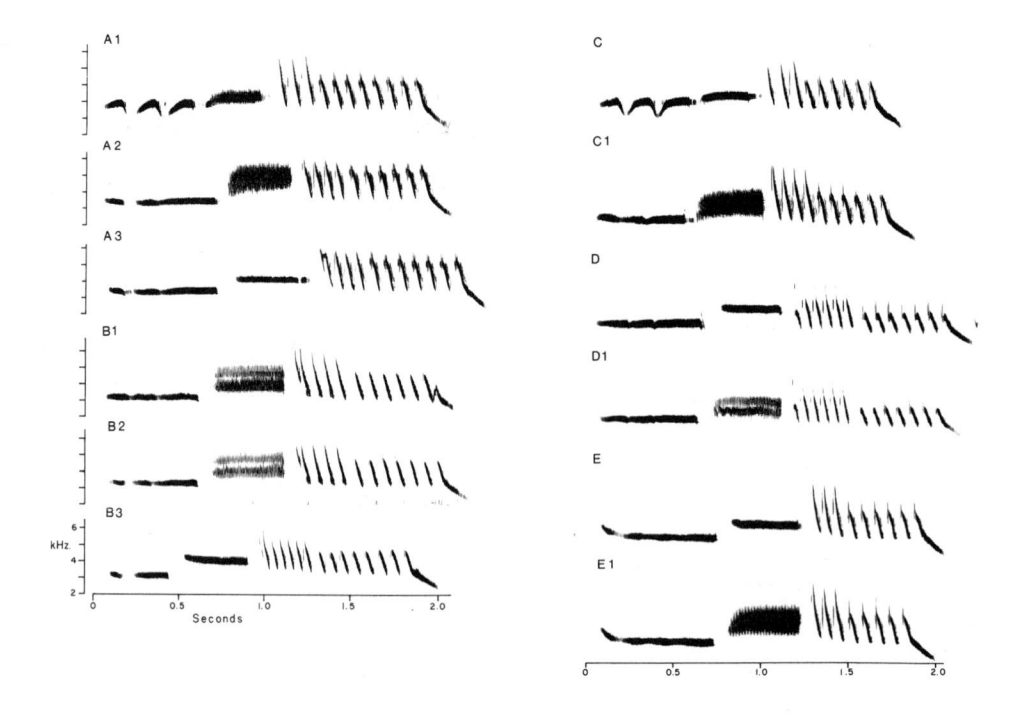

Figure 6. Songs A1 to A3 are three themes from an individual with a trivalent repertoire recorded at El Cerrito. The rest of the motifs are from birds with bivalent repertoires. See text for fuller explanation of figure.

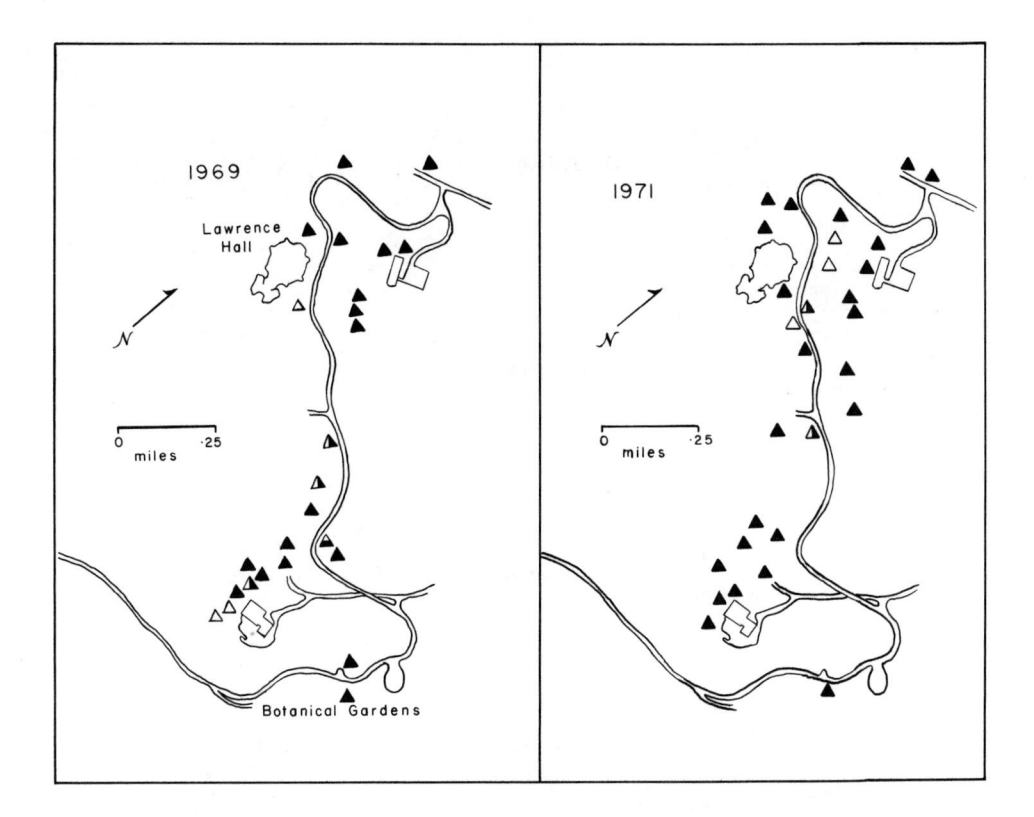

Figure 7. Map of Strawberry Canyon, east of the University of California campus. White triangles represent birds singing Berkeley themes, and black triangles are individuals singing Tilden themes. Black and white triangles divided vertically represent "cultural hybrids." The one black and white triangle divided horizontally is a bird singing both themes recorded at that spot in 1968. All the rest of the birds were recorded in 1969.

Figure 8. Strawberry Canyon in 1971. Symbols used as in figure 7. Note changes in the distribution of song types.

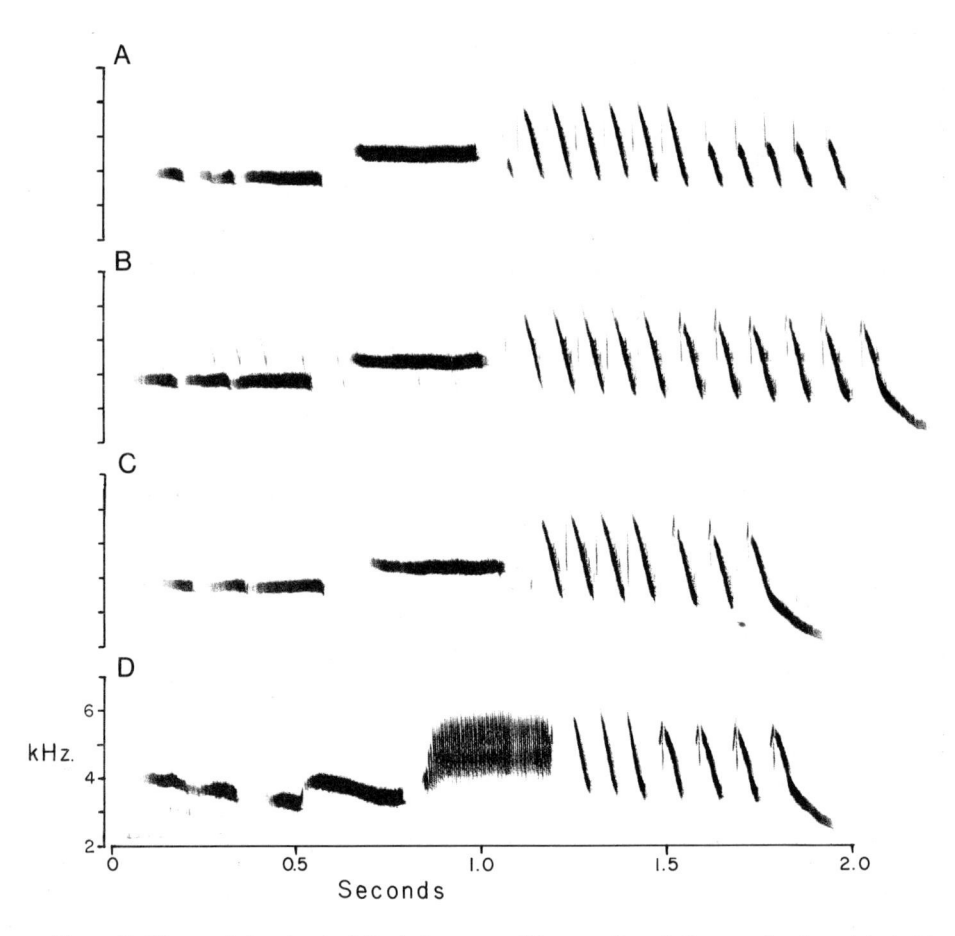

Figure 9. Theme A is a typical Berkeley song. Themes B and C are of cultural hybrid songs recorded in Strawberry Canyon, both sung by the same bird. Theme D is a typical Tilden song sung by the same individual that sang song A.

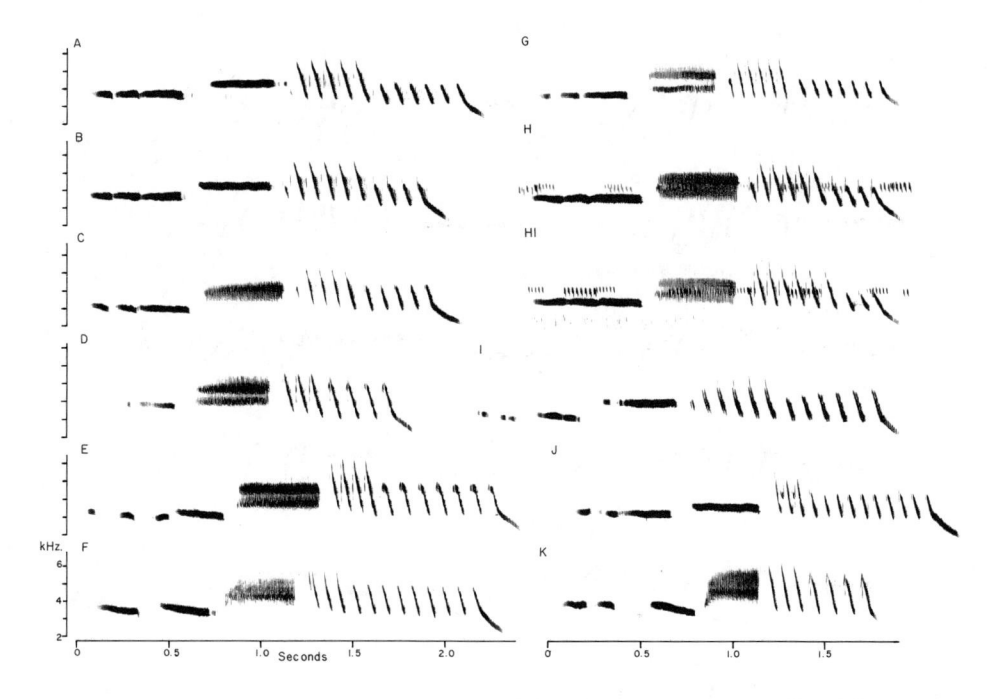

Figure 10. Tilden and Berkeley themes recorded in Strawberry Canyon and the Berkeley Hills. Themes D to F and Theme I are cultural hybrid songs. See text for fuller explanation of figure.

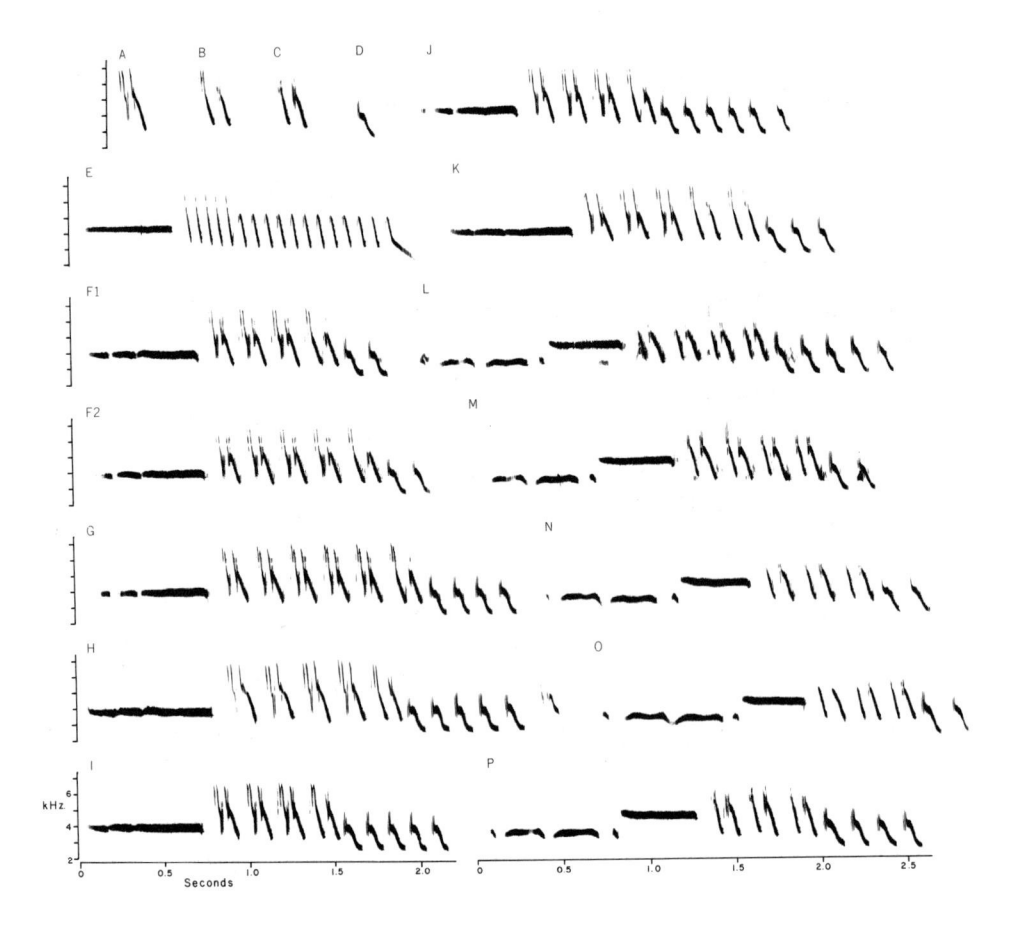

Figure 11. Variation in themes recorded on Brooks Island. A to D are syllables encountered in Brooks Island themes. E is a typical Berkeley theme for comparison. Songs F1 to K are one-whistled songs and L to P are two-whistled songs. Song H terminates with a call note.

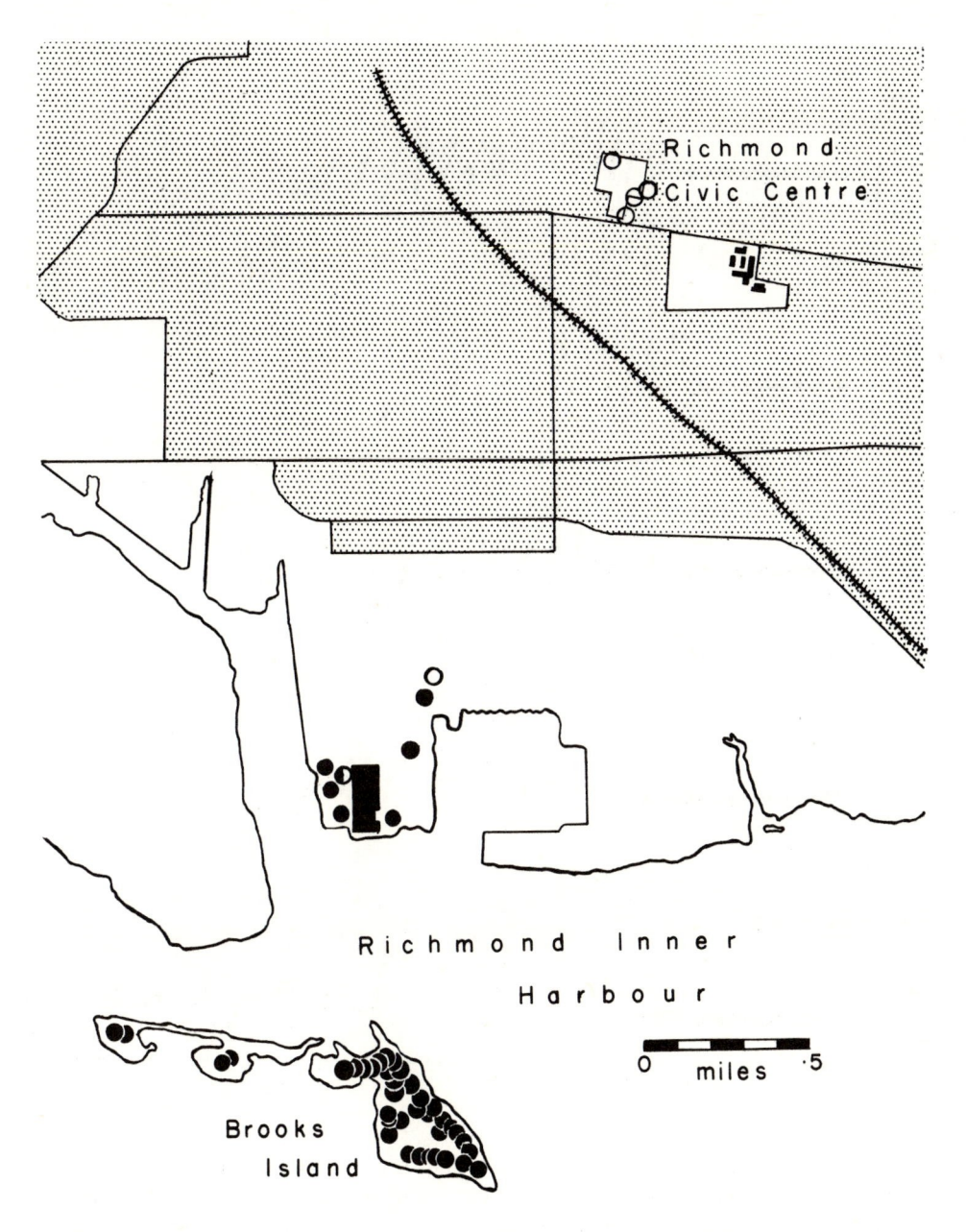

Figure 12. Map showing the relationship of Brooks Island to the Richmond mainland and the distribution of song themes; open circles indicate Berkeley themes, black spots indicate Brooks Island themes, and the one-half blackened dot indicates a "cultural hybrid."

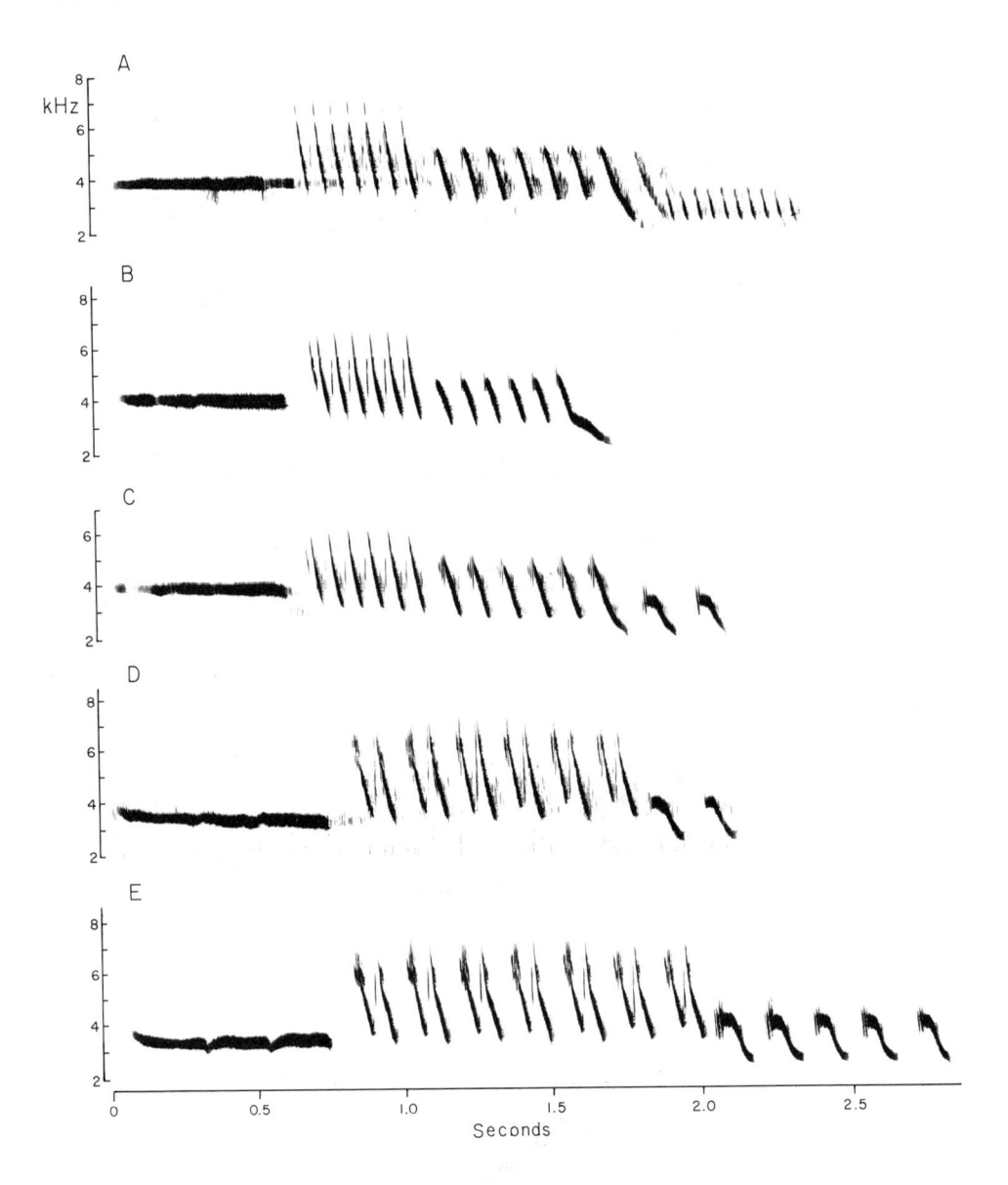

Figure 13. A and B are Berkeley themes. Song C is a "cultural hybrid" between the Berkeley and Brooks Island themes. Songs D and E are variants of the Brooks Island theme recorded on the Richmond mainland.

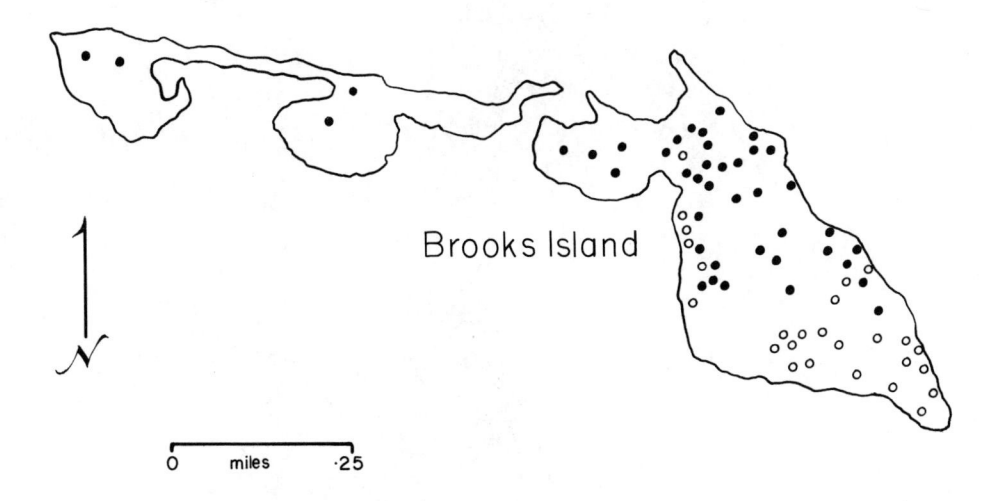

Figure 14. Map of Brooks Island showing the distribution of the two subdialects. Each black dot indicates a bird that sang a one-whistled theme, and each clear circle the singing post of a bird that sang a two-whistled song. Note that the two song types are essentially allopatric in distribution.

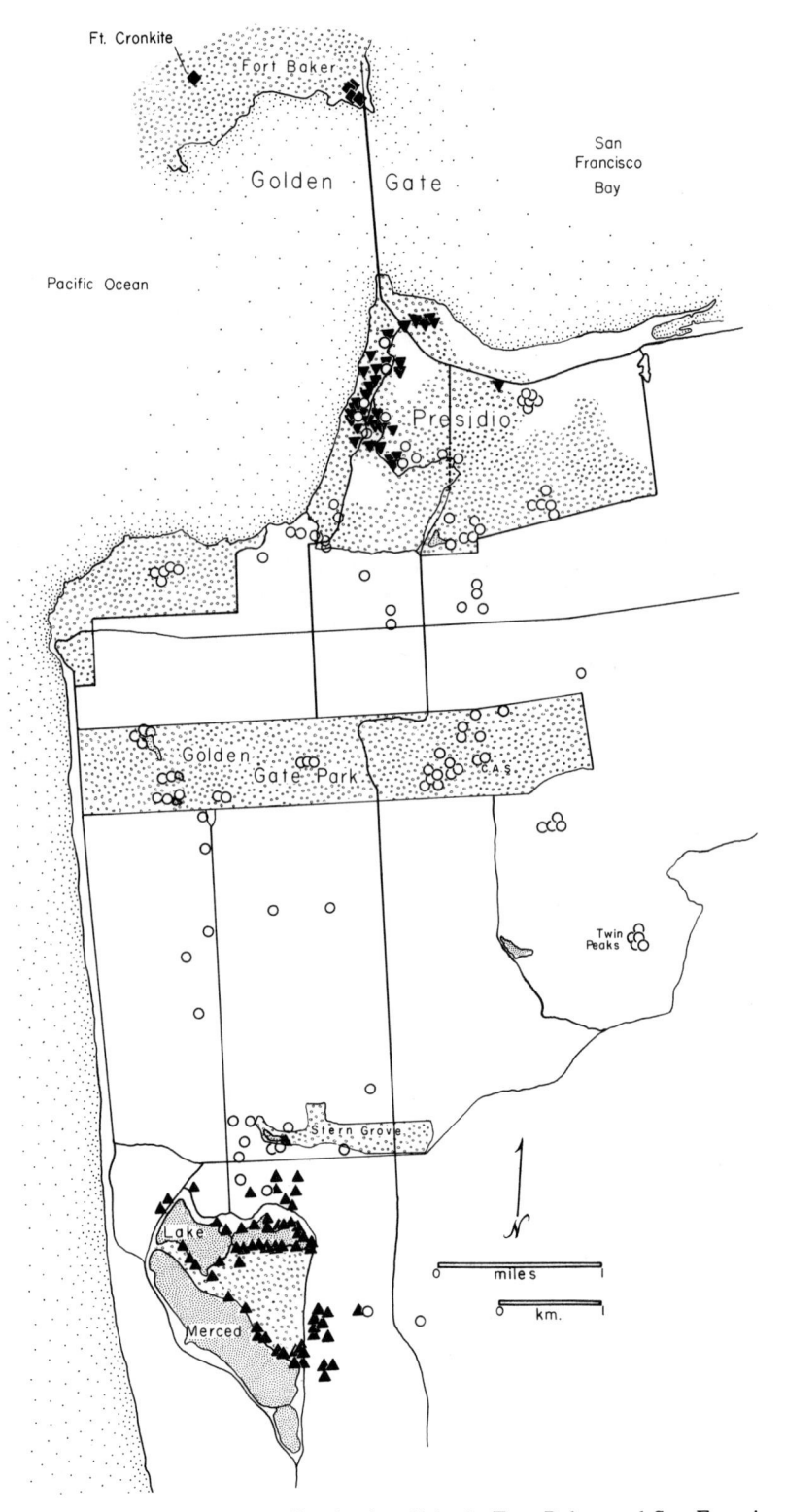

Figure 15. Map showing song collecting localities in Fort Baker and San Francisco. Black diamonds indicate birds singing Fort Baker songs; inverted black triangles are birds singing Presidio themes; clear circles indicate San Francisco themes and black triangles Lake Merced themes.

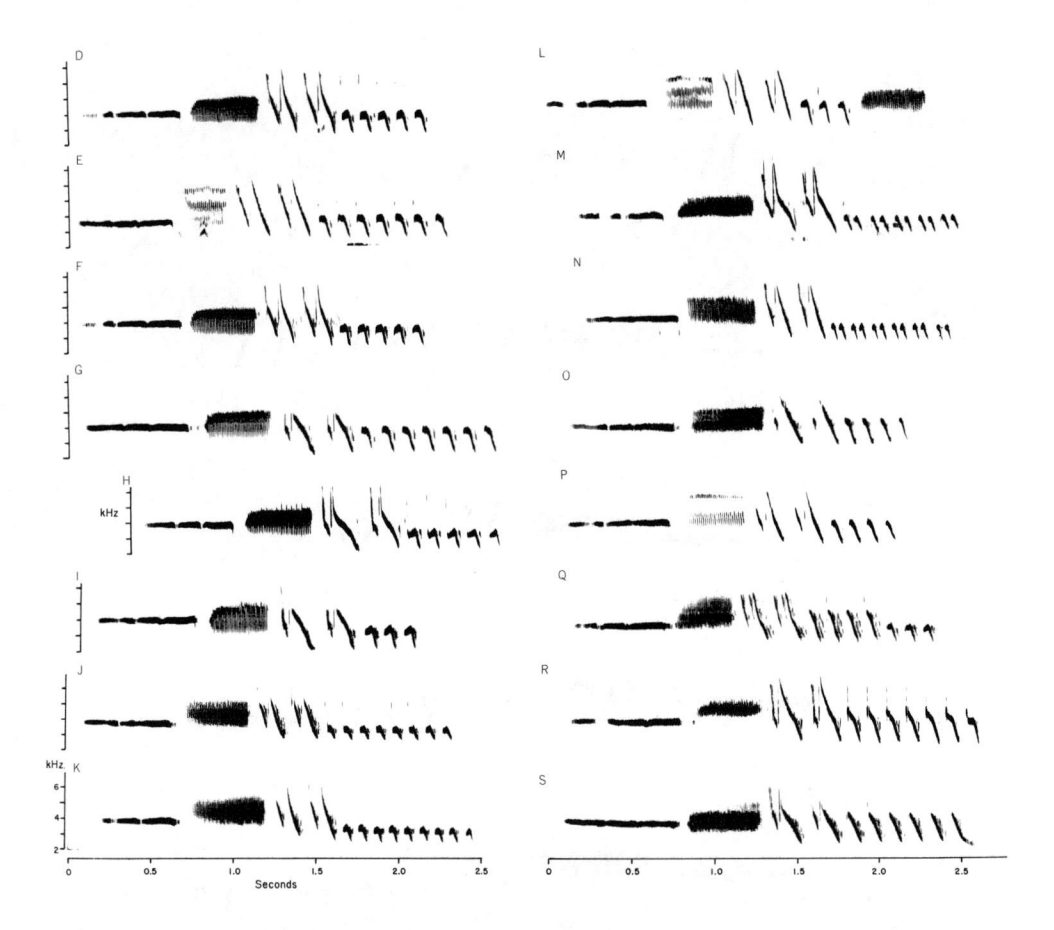

Figure 16. D to N illustrate variation in Presidio songs. Songs O to R are cultural hybrids between motifs typical of San Francisco and those typical of the Presidio. Song S is a San Francisco theme for comparison. See text for fuller explanation of figure.

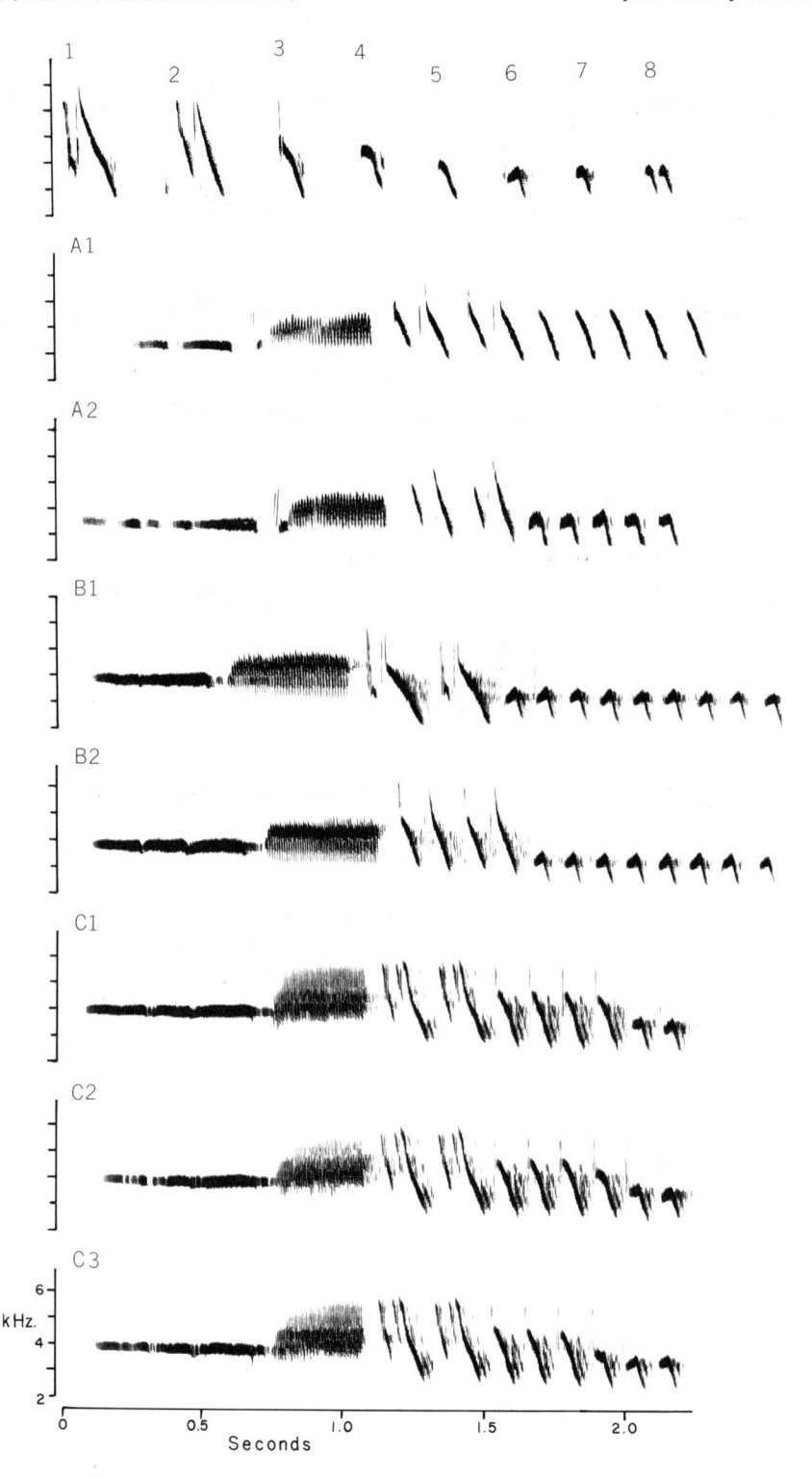

Figure 17. Nos. 1 to 8 are syllable types encountered in Presidio themes. A1 is a San Francisco theme and A2 is a Presidio motif sung by a bird with a bivalent repertoire. Themes B1 and B2 are two songs from the repertoire of another bivalent individual: note different complex syllables in each motif. Songs C1 to C3 are cultural hybrid themes all from the repertoire of one bird. Note that the third to last syllable changes gradually in morphology from type 3 in song C1 to type 4 in song C3.

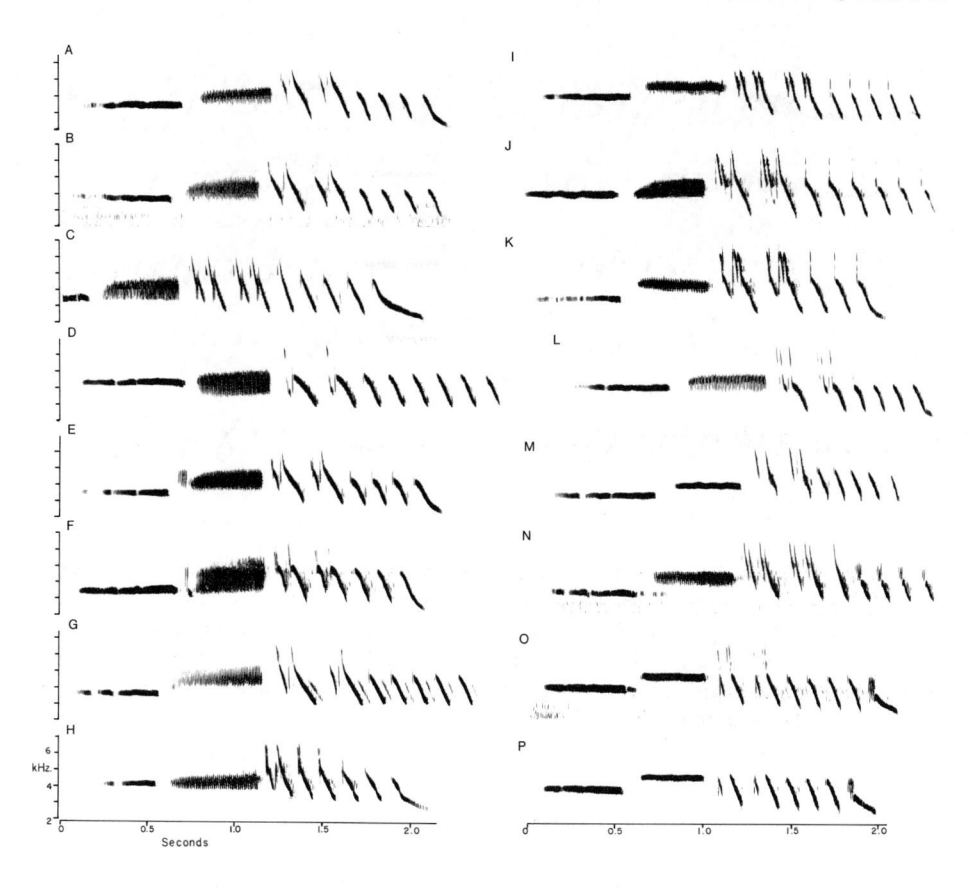

Figure 18. Songs A to P are San Francisco city themes. See text for fuller explanation of figure.

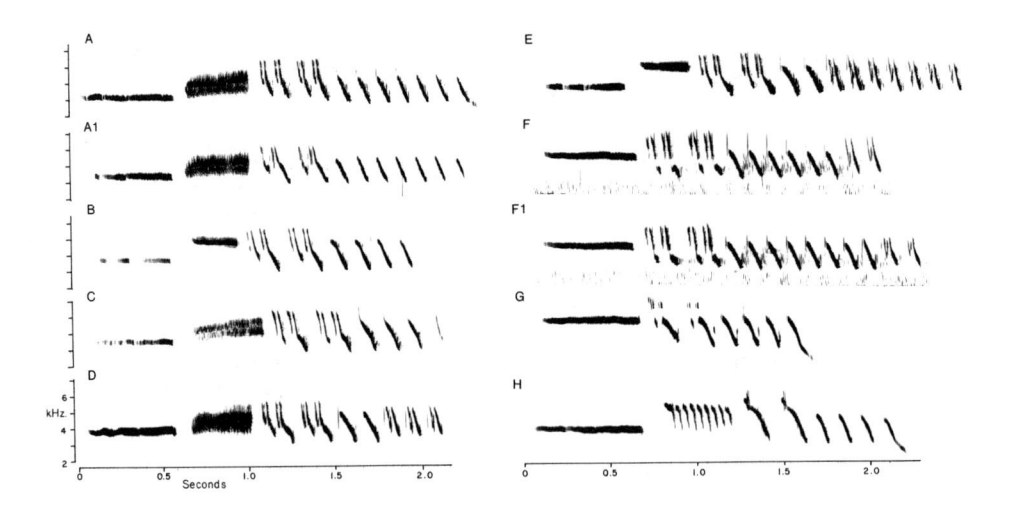

Figure 19. Songs A to F recorded near the California Academy of Sciences, San Francisco, California. Note complex (paired) syllables terminating songs C to F1 which are absent in songs A, A1, and B. Songs G and H were recorded in residential areas in San Francisco. Song G lacks a second phrase and the second phrase in song H is a staccato. Songs F and F1 both from the same bird, also lack second phrases. Songs A and A1 are also two motifs from one individual.

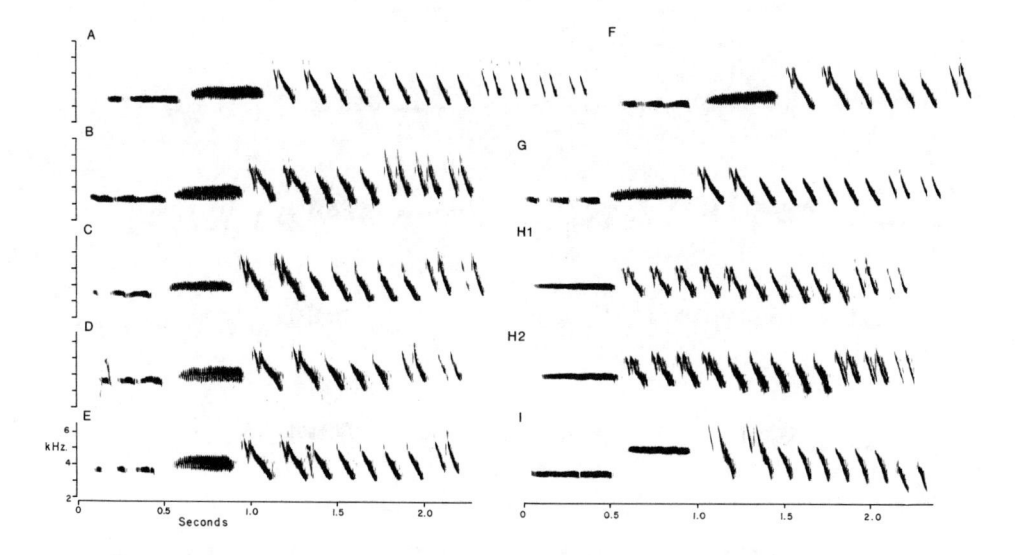

Figure 20. Songs A to H2 recorded in Union Square, San Francisco; note the simple paired syllables terminating these songs. The terminal paired syllables are absent from song I which was recorded at Telegraph Hill, San Francisco.

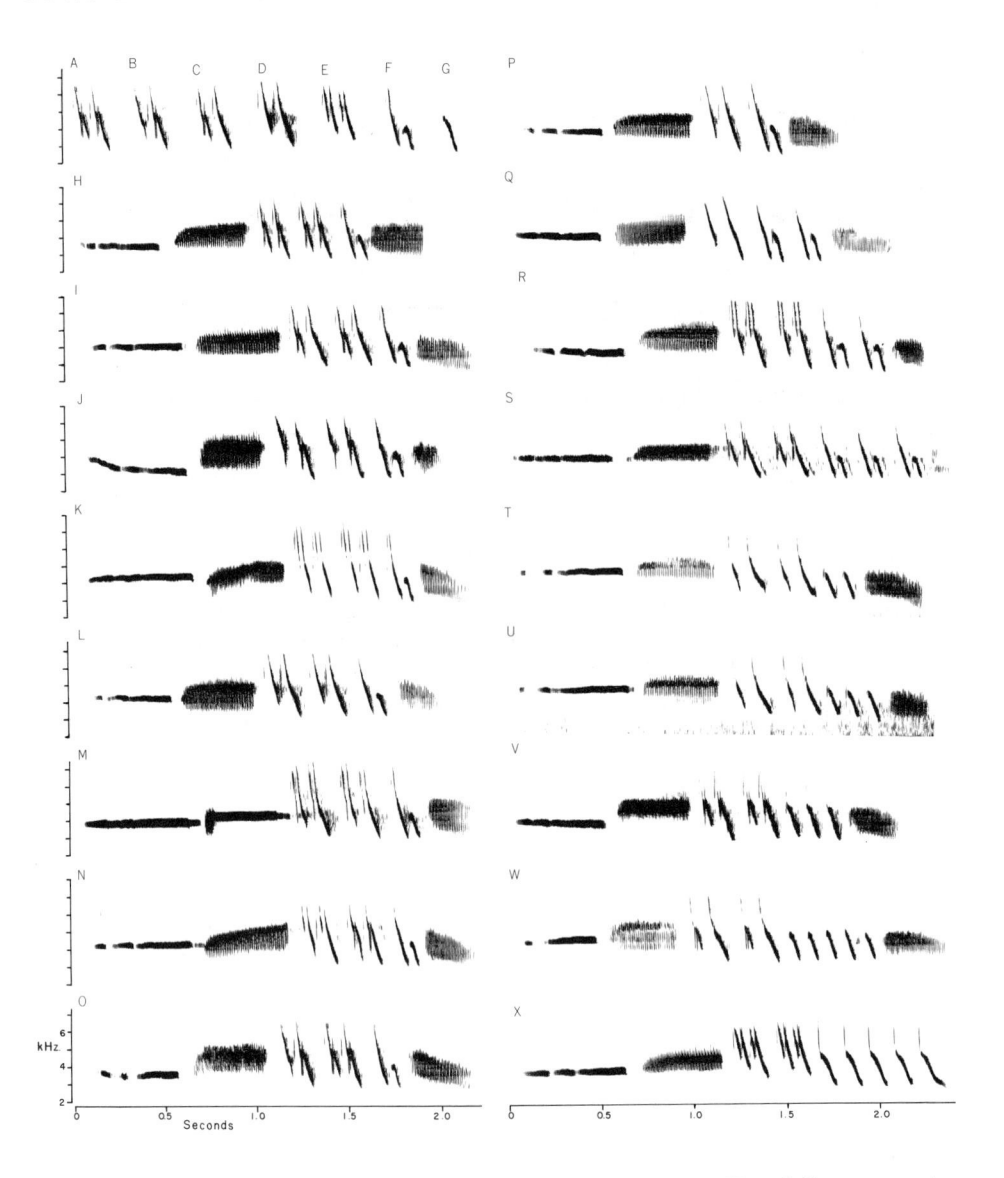

Figure 21. A to G are syllables recorded at Lake Merced. Songs H to S illustrate variation in Lake Merced themes: Note the permutations and combinations of the various syllables illustrated as types A to G. Songs T to W are cultural hybrids and song X is a typical San Francisco theme for comparison.

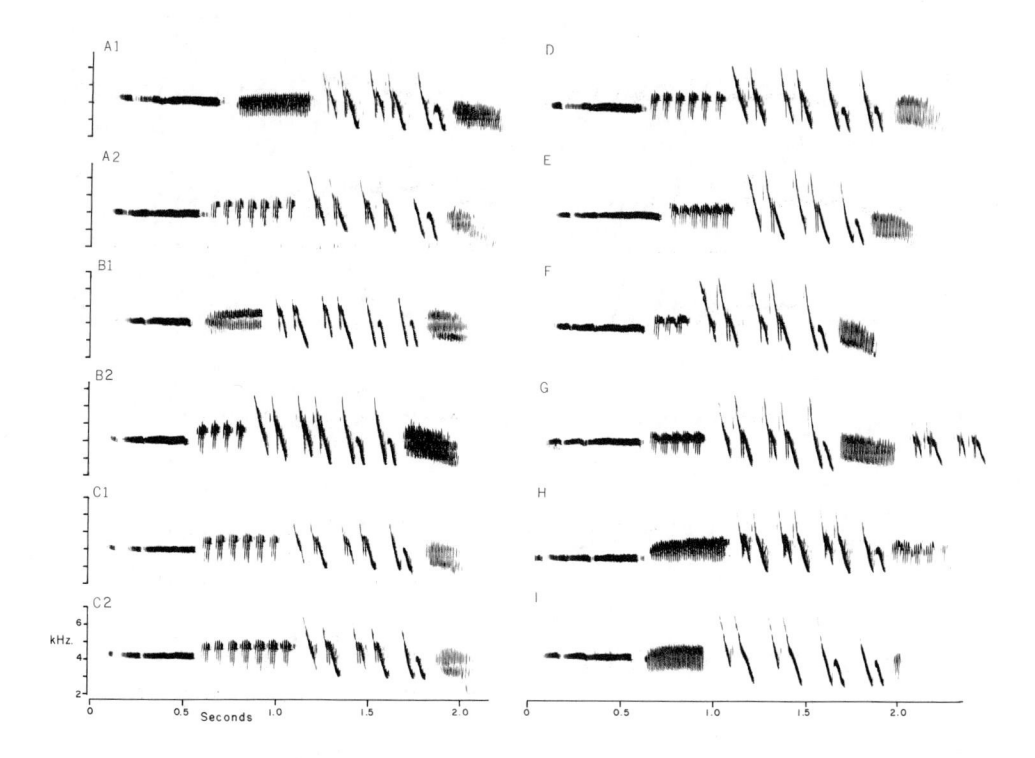

Figure 22. Themes recorded at Lake Merced, San Francisco. A1 and A2 are two themes sung by an individual with a bivalent repertoire. B1 and B2 are two themes from another bird that sang two song types. The second phrases in songs A1 and B1 are buzzes. The second phrases in themes A2 and B2 and C1 to G are staccatos. In songs H and I the terminal phrases are staccatos. See text for fuller explanation of figure.

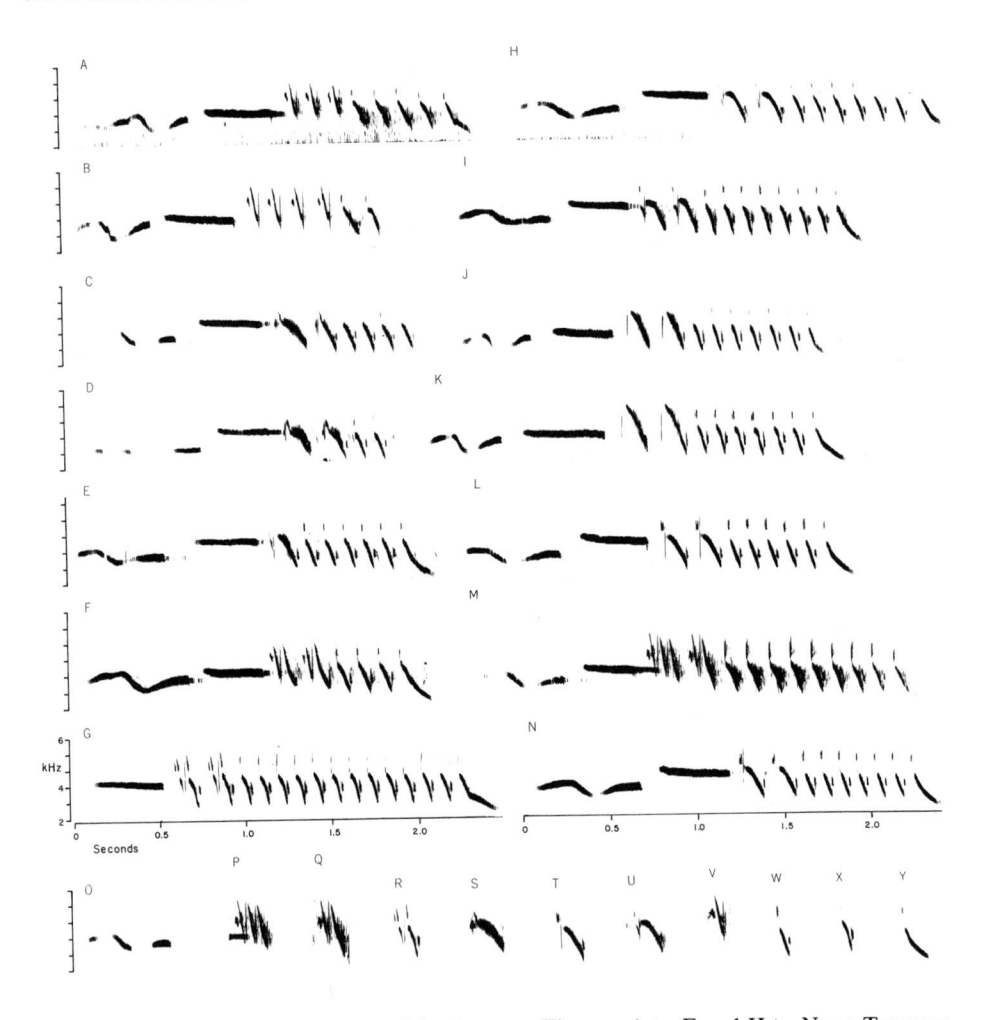

Figure 23. Variation in Treasure Island songs. Themes A to F and H to N are Treasure Island themes with two whistles in the introduction. G is a song with only one whistle from this locality. O is a typical introductory whistle from this locality: Note the amplitude modulation which shows as three dark areas on the spectograms. P to V are complex syllables, and W to Y are simple syllables found in these themes.

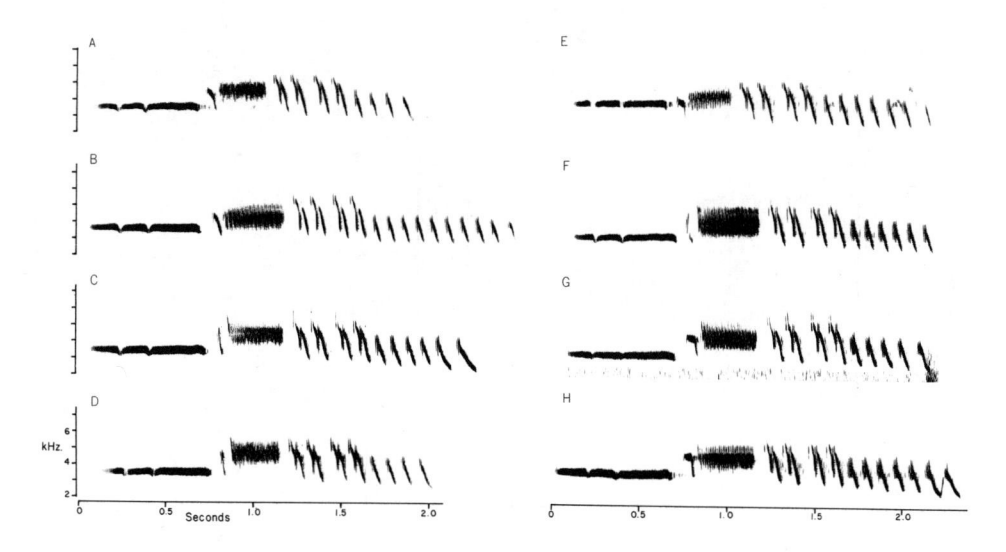

Figure 24. Song samples from Fort Baker, Marin County, California.

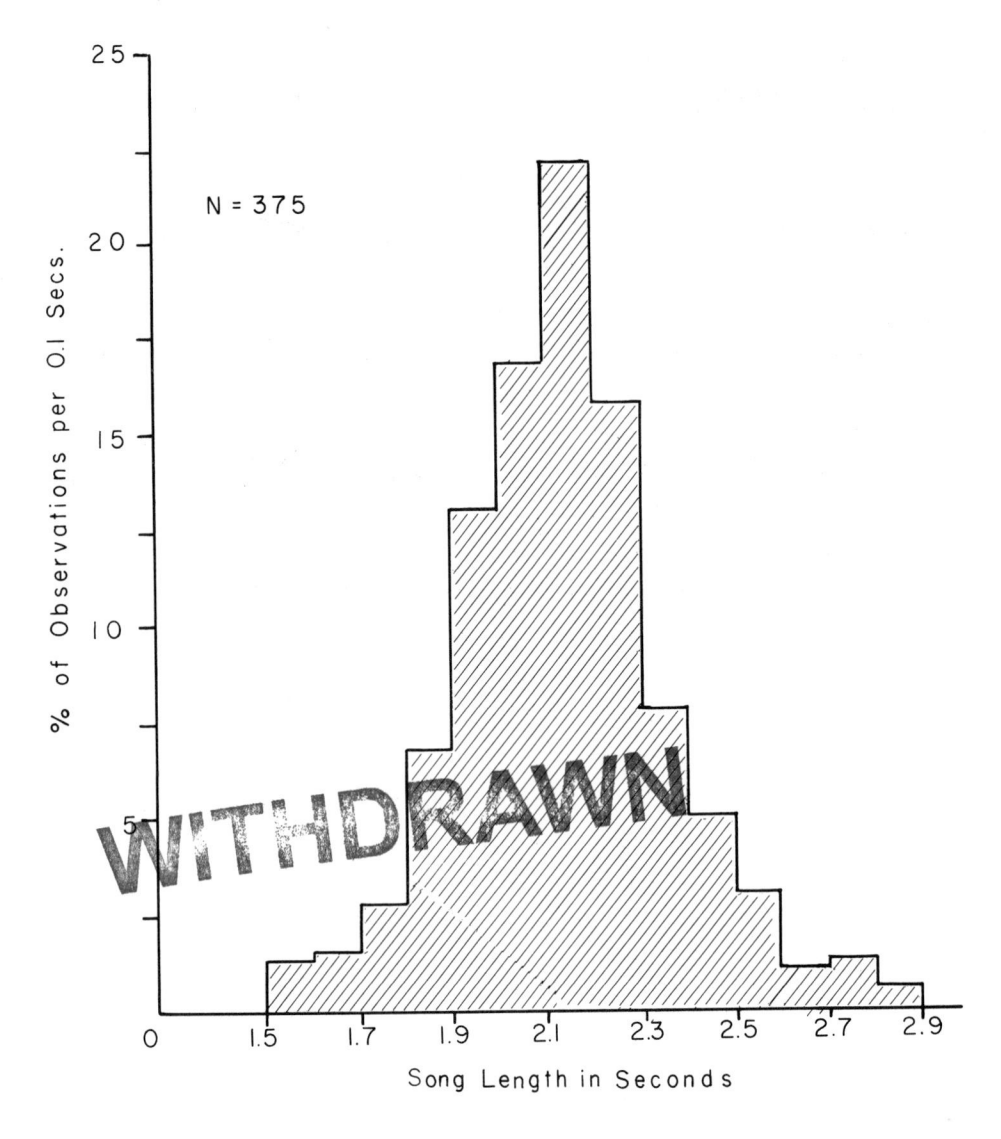

Figure 25. Histogram showing the frequency distribution of the song lengths of 375 White-crowned Sparrows.